Learning English

PASSWORD TO SKYLINE PLUS

Lesebuch zur Einführung in
die Oberstufenarbeit

Herausgegeben von

Sabine Kranz
Arno Paland
Thomas Tepe

Ernst Klett Verlag
Stuttgart Düsseldorf Leipzig

Learning English

Password to Skyline Plus

Herausgegeben von
OStR Sabine Kranz, Köln; StD Arno Paland, Mülheim/Ruhr; StD Thomas Tepe, Münster
unter Mitarbeit von StD Arthur Winter, Unna.

Weitere Mitarbeit
StR Heinz-Günther Böhne, Köln; StD Werner Buddenkotte, Münster; StR Dr. Hans Georg Kotthoff, Köln; StD Antje Malycha, Kierspe; StD Friedhold Schmidt, Köln; StD T. Lothar Wullen, Bergisch Gladbach.

Beratende Mitarbeit
StD Elke Barausch-Hummes, Köln; StD Christin Grieser-Kindel; StD Detlef Kunz, Wuppertal.

Tonträger zu *Password to Skyline Plus*

Inhaltsidentisch mit den Tonträgern der bisherigen Fassung.

Kassette mit ausgewählten Texten und Liedern sowie den Hörverstehenstexten.
Klettnummer 510432

CD mit dem gleichen Inhalt wie die Kassette.
Klettnummer 510435

Password to Skyline Plus Workbook 510462

1. Auflage 1 15 14 13 12 | 2011 2010 2009 2008

Alle Drucke dieser Auflage können im Unterricht nebeneinander benutzt werden,
sie sind untereinander unverändert.
Die letzte Zahl bezeichnet das Jahr dieses Druckes.

Internetadresse: www.klett-verlag.de

Redaktion: Louise Carleton, M.A., Helen Smyth, B.A., Dr. Hartmut K. Selke

Umschlag und Grafik: Christian Dekelver, Weinstadt.
Layout: Arno Kämpgen, Münster.
Druck: Firmengruppe APPL, aprinta druck, Wemding
Printed in Germany.

ISBN 3-12-510460-2

9 783125 104600

Contents

Read me!

When you open this book, you'll find material taken from different sources – literature, newspapers, films, soap operas, songs, statistics, cartoons – that people all over the English-speaking world also read or listen to, watch and laugh about. The theme of this book is 'growing up', so you'll see what young people from other countries have to say about this topic. In the activities marked with a "●" you'll be able to talk about your own experiences, and make comparisons with your own situation. Whenever you do this, have a look at the phrases on page 119 – they will help you to express yourself.

At the back of the book, there are *strategy pages* which contain useful tips and techniques to help you do the activities in the book. They have been divided into different categories to make them easier to use. They also contain ideas for projects which will make learning English more fun.

Reading authentic texts is not always easy as you'll sometimes come across words that are new to you. Don't worry, nobody can know all the words in the English language. To help you become more independent we have included tips in the *strategy pages* – e.g. how to use an English-English dictionary, how to survive without a dictionary – to help you find out the meaning of new words yourselves. As it is important for you to practise using these techniques, we have not explained all the unknown words. We also suggest that you read texts in groups or with a partner – learning together is more fun and you can then also help each other. If you need any extra help practising new skills and vocabulary, you can refer to your *Password to Skyline Plus Workbook* – cross-references are given in special boxes throughout the book.

It is also important to actively learn new words. The more words and structures you have, the better you'll be able to communicate. As you are now an advanced learner of English we don't always tell you to do this – it's up to you. So when you read the texts, note down any English words and phrases you find interesting and useful. There are tips on how to do this on the *strategy page* "Learning vocabulary".

There are two glossaries on pages 124–126 – one of literary terms and the other of audio-visual terms. Terms which appear in the coloured boxes throughout the book have been listed here alphabetically for easy reference.

We wish you success and a lot of fun with *Password to Skyline Plus!*

Your *Password to Skyline Plus* Team

Erklärung der Abkürzungen und Symbole

•S•	text also on cassette and CD
•L•	Listening comprehension text on cassette and CD
WB	*Password to Skyline Plus Workbook*
AE	American English
arch.	archaic
b.	born
BE	British English
cf.	compare, see
e.g.	for example
etc.	et cetera, and so on

fig.	figurative
i.e.	that is
l.; ll.	line; lines
opp. of	opposite of
o.s.	oneself
p.; pp.	page; pages
s.o.	someone
s.th.	something
usu.	usually
⚠	be careful – false friend
●	possible pre-/post-reading activity
US	refers to a specifically American phenomenon

What kind of learner am I?

Before you start working with this book, you may find it useful to reflect on your language learning experiences up to now. Once, you are aware of the learning methods you find most effective or prefer, you could consider new ways of improving your learning skills.

Getting started ▶

- a) Take five minutes to think about your learning experiences up to now. You can think of areas outside of school, too. Which experiences would you describe as difficult and unproductive? Which experiences were positive and productive? Try to write down one or two reasons as to why this was the case.
  b) In groups, compare your experiences. Then, try to suggest ways in which the learning experiences could have been made more productive or easier.

Now look at the following analysis.
For each of the following types score yourself 0, 1, 2, or 3 in the brackets to show how you like to learn best.

0 = no; 1 = occasionally; 2 = usually; 3 = yes

Type 1

❑ I like to learn by watching and listening to native speakers.
❑ I like to learn by talking to friends in English.
❑ At home, I like to learn by watching TV and/or videotapes in English.
❑ I like to learn by using English out of class.
❑ I like to learn English words by hearing them.
❑ I like to learn by having conversations.

Total ❑

Type 2

❑ I like the teacher to explain everything to us.
❑ I want to write everything in my notebook.
❑ I like to have my own textbook.
❑ In class, I like to learn by reading.
❑ I like to study grammar.
❑ I like to learn English words by seeing them.

Total ❑

Type 3

❑ In class, I like to learn by playing games.
❑ In class, I like to learn by looking at pictures, films and videotapes.
❑ I like to learn English by talking in pairs.
❑ At home, I like to learn by using audiotapes.
❑ In class, I like to listen to and use audiotapes.
❑ I like to go out with the class and practise English.

Total ❑

Type 4
I like to study grammar. ❑
At home, I like to learn by studying English books. ❑
I like to study English by myself (alone). ❑
I like the teacher to let me find my mistakes. ❑
I like the teacher to give us problems to work on. ❑
At home, I like to learn by reading newspapers. ❑

❑ Total

Add up your score for each section and put the number in the Total box. The highest total shows what kind of learner you are.

Look at the descriptions below:

The communicator

Type 1: If you have a high score in this section, you are probably a good communicator. You enjoy interacting with people and using the English you have learned in a natural way.

The teacher-oriented learner

Type 2: If you have a high score in this section, you probably enjoy learning English in class. You like the teacher to lead you through learning the language.

The group learner

Type 3: If you have a high score in this section, you probably enjoy learning English by examples. You like learning with other people and you see learning English as fun.

The independent learner

Type 4: If you have a high score in this section, you probably like learning English by studying it in detail. You like to work by yourself and find out how to use the language on your own.

A step further

- You may find that you do not fit neatly into any one of the above categories. If so, write out the statements that are most true for you, then try to write a description of yourself as a language learner.
- Look at the items you have scored with 0. Can you explain why you do not like doing these activities?
- What do you do in place of these activities? Discuss your thoughts with a partner, other group members, or your teacher.
- Just for fun! If the type of learner you are, was a particular animal, what kind would you be? Draw this animal and write down a few adjectives or phrases which describe how you learn, e.g. lion, a leader; a snail, slow but sure; an elephant, forgets nothing…

Tasks for Independent Language Learning (What's my style?) by D. Nunan, David Gardner & Lindsay Miller (eds.) VA: TESOL, 1996.

SUPERMAN

- Choose the photo which appeals to you most and say why.
- Describe the people in the pictures. What sort of situation are they in? What do their faces and posture tell you about their feelings? Which of the photos tells you something about the family background and interests of these young people?
- What might the young people have been thinking at the time the photograph was taken?
- If these photos were to be shown at an exhibition, what titles would you suggest for them?
- Several years later the girls and boys show their photo to a close friend. What might they say about the photo?
- Which of these photos is most likely to be from a film? What do you think the film would be about, and in what scene would this photo fit?
- What do you think each of these young people might be doing in ten years' time?

WB: p. 9, "Celebrity quiz"; p. 10, In five years' time; p. 21, Outward appearances

Chapter one

Family ties

Growing up?

Before you read

Simile
A comparison between two objects or ideas, using "like", "as" or "as if".

- a) According to your parents, did you have any bad habits when you were younger? What did they complain about most?
  b) What are their main points of criticism today?
- a) Read the first *simile*. Then complete the remaining sentences with your own explanations.

  Life is like a tin of sardines – we're all looking for the key.
  Life is like a battlefield – …
  Life is like a bowl of cherries – …
  Life is like a river – …

  Now make up a simile of your own, explaining what life is like.
  b) Make up some more similes. What are the world, school, childhood and growing up like?

Growing up?

It must be, oooh,
a month or more
since they last complained
about the way I eat
or crisps I drop
on the kitchen floor
or not washing my feet
or the TV left on
when I go out
or the spoon clunking
against my teeth
or how loudly I shout
or my unmade bed,
mud on the stair,
soap left to drown
or the state of my hair …
It must be
a month or more.
Have they given up
in despair?
For years
they've nagged me
to grow up,
to act my age.
Can it be
that it's happened,
that I'm ready
to step out of my cage?

10 **to clunk** to hit (of hard objects)

15 **to drown** to die in water because you cannot breathe

20 **despair** feeling that everything is wrong and will never get better

22 **to nag s.o.** to complain to s.o. in an irritating way

By Wes Magee, *Morning Break and Other Poems,* Cambridge: Cambridge University Press, 1989.

Reading and thinking

1. Briefly say what the poem is about.
2. How does the picture reflect what is said in the poem?
3. a) What do you learn about the *speaker?*
   b) How would you describe the parents and their relationship with the speaker?
4. a) Which of these adjectives best describe the way the speaker feels? Why?
   ironic – sad – angry – thoughtful – misunderstood
   frustrated – resigned – optimistic – surprised
   b) Read the poem aloud in an appropriate manner (think of tone, speed, etc.).
5. What makes this text a poem? On the other hand, what makes it difficult to see as a poem?

Speaker
The speaker is the voice speaking to us in a poem. He/she is not necessarily identical with the author, even if "I" is used.

A step further

- When would you say that a person is truly 'grown up'? What rights and responsibilities does this involve? Give as many definitions as possible, then try to agree on the best one.
- Write a parallel poem (see page 118) from the parents' perspective. You may decide to change the title but your poem should:
  - have the same beginning: "It must be, ... since he/she ...";
  - be similar in structure;
  - end with a question and something *symbolic.*
- Rewrite the poem as a letter to a friend. See page 118 for help.
- Later that day, the parents are talking about the speaker. In pairs, write their dialogue. Half the class should assume that they have indeed "given up in despair", the other half should show them discussing new ideas and ways of dealing with their son/daughter. Present your dialogue to the rest of the class.

Symbol
Something concrete (an object, a place, etc.) which stands for an abstract idea, e.g. a rose is a symbol of love.

WB: p. 11, Afraid of what he might do/ Annoying situations; p. 13, Nagging

"Saying the bogeyman will get him doesn't seem to have too much effect these days."

Could the young man be the speaker in the poem? Why, why not?

bogeyman imaginary evil man

Keep on running

Before you read ▶

- Look at the picture.
  a) What do you think is the connection between the woman and the girl?
  b) What do you think has just happened, and why?
  c) Imagine the girl now turns around. What do you think the woman and girl say to each other? In pairs, write their dialogue.
- a) One character in the extract says: "I make the decisions in this house." Who do you think is speaking to whom? In what situation? What similar things have been said to you?
  b) In groups of two or three, prepare a *sketch* which contains the above sentence. Think of a suitable situation or conflict, distribute the roles and, as a group, develop a dialogue with an effective ending. Practise the sketch and act it out in class. See page 117 for further help. See also WB: pp. 45–46, "How to hold a conversation" 1 and 2.

Sketch
A short humorous scene often as part of a theatre or television show.

▶ *When you read the following text, look up any words you do not know in your English dictionary. You'll find help on page 108.*

[At Jackie's *house that afternoon after school...]*

Jackie *(laughing)* Oh mum, [...] Guess what happened today.

Mum Something nice was it?

Jackie Brilliant.

Mum Must be to do with running then. What is it?

Jackie They've chosen me to run for the County in the National Cross Country finals in Brighton.

Mum That's lovely, pet. Running for the County, eh. Well love, nobody deserves it more than you do, all that training you do. All those miles you run every week. If anybody deserves something like that you do.

Jackie I'm so nervous already I can hardly keep still.

8 **pet** *(informal) here:* dear, darling

MUM Your dad'll be so proud, love. But you'll have to keep calm and get plenty of rest or you'll not be fit for it. Come on, let's celebrate. I'll make a cup of tea. *(She starts to make the tea, filling the kettle.)* When is it love? We shall all be there to watch.

JACKIE Saturday, mum.

MUM Not next Saturday, Jackie?

JACKIE Yes, next Saturday afternoon. Why?

MUM Not next Saturday, Jack. We're going away next weekend!

JACKIE *(stunned)* Going away? No one said anything to me about going away. Where to?

MUM It was to be a surprise for you and Bobby. We've arranged to go to Norfolk to stay with Uncle Norman and Aunty Betty. Your dad fixed it up weeks ago.

JACKIE *(wailing)* Well, I didn't know.

MUM They've just got a new pony and trap, and some calves and lambs to fatten.

JACKIE But it's the National finals, mum. I can't miss them. Can't you put it off till next week?

MUM I don't know, love. I'll have to ask your dad. He said something about next weekend being definite on account of something to do with some building work at the farm that's due to start. Some alterations Norman and Betty are getting done. Improvements.

JACKIE *(very upset)* Isn't it real! The best thing in my life happens and something spoils it! It's not fair!

MUM There now love, don't cry. We'll see what your dad says when he gets home. Here you are, drink your tea.

[Later that evening.]

DAD So that's how it is, Jackie. Betty and Norman start their alterations next week so your Brighton weekend is the last one they'll have free till God knows when.

JACKIE But it's the National finals, dad. If it were some tinpot little race like most weekends it wouldn't matter, but the National finals ...

DAD I know, Jack. I understand how you feel, but we've got to go and stay with them. He is my step-brother and remember, they haven't got any kids, so whenever something happens to them...

MUM *(shocked)* Don't you be so morbid!

DAD I'm not being morbid, Daphne, but you know as well as I do, they are knocking on a bit now and they haven't got any children of their own. I don't think comparative strangers should step in at the last minute. Not when they've got family.

JACKIE But I've got to go to Brighton, dad. I *must* go.

DAD *(flaring up)* *Got* to go? *Must* go? Who says so? Let me tell you my girl, *I* make the decisions in this house, not one of your teacher friends. When they pay your bills then they can tell you what you've got to do.

JACKIE *(in despair)* None of my teachers said it, dad. I said it because it's something I want to do. I've *got* to do it, dad. It's the biggest thing that ever happened to me.

27 **trap** *here:* light horse-drawn carriage with two wheels

35 **Isn't it real!** *(informal)* Isn't it unfair!

43 **tinpot** *(informal)* unimportant

50 **to be knocking on** *(informal)* to be getting older

65 **'Course** *(informal)* of course

78 **interview** job interview

83 **common** *(negative) here:* lower-class, bad-mannered, uncultured

From *Keep on Running* by Roger Burford-Mason in *Stage Write*, London: Bell & Hyman, 1988, pp. 33–37.

MUM Come on now you two, don't let's quarrel about it. I expect we can find somebody to put Jackie up for the weekend while we go to the farm.

DAD It's not anybody's place to put her up.

MUM 'Course it's not Frank, but it would solve the problem, wouldn't it? You feel we must go to Norfolk for the weekend and Jackie will die if she doesn't run in that race in Brighton. How else are we going to fix it up?

JACKIE *(tearful)* What, go to Brighton by myself? You mean you wouldn't come to watch?

DAD *(crossly)* Have some sense girl. How could we come to Brighton to watch you *and* go to Norfolk? They're at opposite ends of the country. I wash my hands of it. If you want to go to Brighton you'll have to go without us. Me, I think you're daft to pass up a weekend at your Aunty Betty's for a couple of hours running.

JACKIE *(angrily)* Well you would, wouldn't you. You've never even tried to understand it. It won't get me a job. It won't get me any 'O' levels. It won't count at an interview. I don't suppose it matters that it's one of the few things I am good at and that lots of people think I could have a really good future running. If it doesn't put anything in a wage packet, you don't want to know!

MUM *(sharply)* Jackie! Don't you speak to your father like that. He's not one of your common classmates.

JACKIE My classmates may be common but at least they care about me. More than he does! I'm going to bed. Good night! *(She slams out of the room.)*

Reading and thinking

Talking about behaviour in conflicts

A person may be...
authoritarian • selfish
angry • understanding
impatient • emotional
short-tempered • sensitive
narrow-minded

to hit the roof
to sulk
to calm s.o. down
to fly into a fury
to argue sensibly
to make a compromise
to give in to s.o.
to put one's foot down

1. a) Look up the following words in your dictionary. Find the correct word class and the meaning which fits the context. If given, note down synonyms. See page 108 for help.
   cross (ll. 6, 71), deserves (l. 9), celebrate (l. 14), stunned (l. 21), fixed up (l. 25), wailing (l. 26), put off (l. 29), alteration (l. 34), spoils (l. 36), morbid (l. 48), step in (l. 51), quarrel (l. 61), put s.o. up (l. 62), daft (l. 74), pass up (l. 74)
   b) In a few sentences, sum up what the text is about. Do not use the words/phrases above or the words explained in the annotations.
2. a) Divide the text into sections. Find headings for each of them.
   b) Would you have preferred a different title for the text? Why, why not?
3. What conflict does the text describe? Compare the different interests of the characters in this situation. What arguments do they use?
4. How do the characters behave in this situation? Trace their behaviour through the text. Use the phrases on the left.
5. You can visualize the 'constellation of characters' in this extract through a triangle in which the position of the characters and the thickness of the connecting lines show the quality of the relationships.
   Do you think the triangle on the next page reflects the family constellation in the text? If not, draw a better triangle on the board and explain it to the class. Back up your statements with quotations from the text. See page 116.

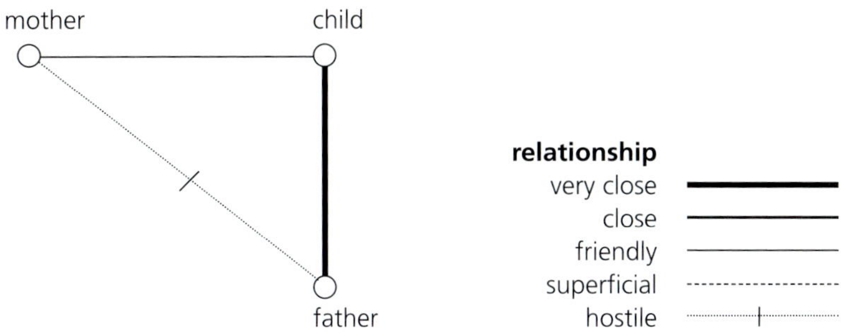

WB: p. 22, Keep on running

◀ Close-up: language

In groups, prepare a text on:
a) what Jackie is allowed to do or forbidden to do by her parents;
b) what rules Jackie might dream of giving her parents to get her revenge.
Leave out the auxiliaries for the other groups to fill in under your supervision. Then have them rewrite your texts in the past tense.

◀ A step further

- Look at the picture on page 12. Do you think this could be Jackie and her mum? Give reasons for your answer.
- a) Rewrite this dramatic text as a *narrative text.* You might want to use reported speech: Check the rules in a grammar and cf. WB: pages 13–14.
  b) What kind of ending seems most likely to you? A surprise ending? An open ending? A happy/unhappy ending? Choose an appropriate ending for your narrative text. See WB: pp. 34–35 for 'plot'/'slice-of-life' stories.
- How would the following characters describe the conflict the next day: Jackie to her best girlfriend? – Dad to Uncle Norman? – Mum to Aunty Betty? See WB: page 26 "Having an argument" for useful expressions.
- On the day after the incident, Jackie writes a letter to her grandmother. She describes the conflict the day before and asks for advice on how to deal with her parents in future. Write this letter, then let your neighbour answer it. See page 118 of this book and WB: page 40 for help.

Narrative text

In a narrative text the author relates an event or a sequence of events. Novels, short stories, etc. are narrative texts; reports and newspaper articles also contain narrative elements.

◀ project

As a *dramatic* text, "Keep on running" is meant to be acted out on stage. Make sure that you are familiar with the words in the box below, then prepare and act out a performance of this text in class. See page 123 for help.

Drama

The author of a *play* (or *drama)* is called a *playwright.* A play may consist of several *acts* which can be subdivided into *scenes.* The *roles* or *parts* are played by *actresses* and *actors,* who make up the *cast.* The *characters* talk to each other in *dialogues.* The *director* helps the actors and actresses to put the *stage directions* (where to stand, how to move and speak) into practice and decides about the use of *props* (furniture or other objects on the stage). A public *performance* is prepared through a number of *rehearsals.* The people who watch the play are called the *audience.* In English, the term drama also refers to the art of writing and performing a play.

WB: p. 17, Who does the work in your family?/ Vocabulary test

Truancy

Before you listen

Talking about excuses

An excuse can be…

- convincing
- believable
- acceptable
- weak
- flimsy
- poor
- ridiculous

Sometimes an excuse…

doesn't convince you
seems far-fetched
doesn't ring true
is impossible to check
is a lie

- a) Look up the words "truant" and "truancy" in a dictionary. Do you know anyone who has ever played truant? Why did they?
  b) How would your parents/teachers react if you played truant?
  c) Write a short letter to your teacher, in which you present an unusual excuse for your absence the day before. Read it out and let the other students judge your excuse. The words and phrases in the box may help you. See WB: page 41 for ideas on how to write a formal letter.

You are going to listen to a dialogue between Terry, a teenager, and his father. Terry has just reached a new level in a complicated video game. His father comes to talk to him, and their dialogue becomes quite heated – the father swears quite a lot. Do not worry if you cannot understand all these expressions, you will still be able to understand the gist of their conversation.
Before you listen to the recording, you should read through the following annotations:

Russell and Bromley chain of shoe shops in Britain
to top o.s. *(informal)* to kill o.s.
headstone stone at the head of one's grave
cherub ['tʃerəb] angel

Listening for gist and tone

Irony
Saying one thing but meaning another.

Sarcasm
Irony which is cutting and meant to hurt.

1. Now listen to the recording without taking any notes. Concentrate on getting a general understanding of the dialogue. Then sum up the conflict in a few sentences.
2. How would you describe the tone in which father and son speak to each other? You could listen to the recording again, collecting examples of different tones.

Talking about tone

The tone in which something is said may be…
friendly • polite • encouraging • playful • humorous • witty • serious
or
ironic • sarcastic • arrogant • angry • provocative • defiant • rude
threatening • rebellious • aggressive

Listening for detail: taking notes

1. Copy this grid into your exercise-book. Listen to the recording again and take notes. See page 111 for help.

	view of school	view of life
Terry's …		
His father's …		

2. Using your notes, write a character portrait of Terry and his father.

◀ **Close-up: register**

1. Thinking about their language, how would you characterize the relationship between father and son?
2. Imagine father and son have improved their relationship and are trying to be nice to each other. Using the notes you have made, rewrite the dialogue choosing a suitable register (see page 121) without changing the conflict. You may, however, decide to change the ending.
   Here are some structures you might want to include:
   "If you keep on nagging, I…"
   "I don't see any point in going to school because…"
   "As school is boring, I…"
   "If you don't have a good education, you…"
   "I am worried about you because…"

◀ project

Find out what your class/friends/family think about video and computer games. Conduct a survey, then present the results to your class. See page 122 for help.
You might also want to find out what people in other countries think about this particular topic. You could, for instance, send a questionnaire to your partner school or ask the pupils to conduct a similar survey and send you the results. Alternatively you might want to ask young people on the Internet to answer the questionnaire.

WB: p. 25, Truancy

"I hate you! You don't understand me and you don't understand my software!"

Cartoons
A cartoon is a drawing in a newspaper/magazine which often deals in a clever and amusing way with something of interest in the news. A cartoon is often made funny by the caption below it.
A strip cartoon or comic strip is a series of drawings that tell a story.

Point out parallels and differences between the *cartoon* and the dialogue "Truancy".

Spock's Guide to Parent Care

Before you read ▶

- Imagine you are the author of a book called *A Parents' Survival Guide*. What would be your FIVE GOLDEN RULES for dealing with teenage children?
- Look at the cartoon below.
  a) What do you think the parents were talking about before they fell asleep?
  b) Continue the baby's monologue.

to drop off *(informal)*
to fall asleep

Close-up: language ▶

1. Before you read the following text, look up the words below in your dictionary (see page 108). Then group them under the headings "parents" or "children", according to which seems more appropriate. Add any others you can think of.
   balky – mature – cocky – suspicious – firm – self-confident
   temper tantrum – to nag – to sulk – nervous breakdown
2. a) Now read "How to survive without a dictionary" on page 108.
   b) Using the techniques listed on page 108, try to guess the meaning of the unknown words in the text below. You will notice that some of the words have been numbered – these numbers will remind you which technique you can use to guess the meaning. To help you, they have been explained again in the box on the left.
   c) In addition, some of the words in the text have been printed in **bold letters** – there is extra help given in the margin.

Surviving without a dictionary
1 refers to *word family*
2 refers to *similar German, French or Latin words*
3 refers to *context*

PARENTS ARE JUST LARGE HUMAN BEINGS. It's only natural for a small child to feel a little **daunted**[3] by the hard work and responsibility of coping[3] with parents. All parents get balky from time to time, and go through phases[2] which worry their children, and all children get tired and discouraged[1] and wonder whether they're doing the right thing.

→ **daunted** How might a small child feel in this situation?

The important thing to remember is that most parents, deep down inside, want nothing more than to be good ones. A parent may act tough and cocky, but at heart he wants to be one of the gang. He wants to learn what's expected of him as a parent and do it. What he needs from you above all is plenty of encouragement, and plenty of **reassurance**[3] that he's doing all right.

→ **reassurance** [ˌrɪə'ʃʊrəns] If he wonders whether he is doing the right thing, what might he need?

EVERY PARENT IS DIFFERENT. This one flies into a fury at the sight of **crayoning**[3] on the wallpaper. That one bursts into tears. Yet another goes into a sulk and won't say anything all afternoon: All these are perfectly normal, healthy reactions. I'd be **inclined** to be suspicious of the parent who seems a little too good to be true. He or she may be **deprived of** emotional experience for **lack of** opportunity. I think I'd ask myself in this case if I was drawing on the wallpaper enough.

THEY AREN'T AS FRAGILE AS THEY LOOK. **Handle**[3] them confidently. Many parents look as though they'll have a nervous breakdown if you bang your toy on the table just once more. Don't worry – nine times out of ten they won't.

DON'T BE AFRAID TO INSIST[2] ON YOUR OWN STANDARDS. There's been a great swing away from the over-permissiveness[1] which used to be the fashion, when a parent's every **whim** was regarded as sacred[2]. Nowadays we've come to realise that on the whole people don't have any very clear ideas about manners[2] or morals until they become parents, when they hastily[2] start to make them up as they go along. They're secretly very grateful for a little firm but tactful[2] guidance[1]. [...]

TEMPER TANTRUMS. Almost all parents have temper tantrums from time to time. You have to remember that between the ages of 20 and 60 parents are going through a difficult phase of their development. They have got to a stage in their exploration[1] of the world at which they find it is rather smaller than they thought. They are discovering the surprising limitations[1] of their personality, and learning to be dependent. It's natural enough for them to want to explode at times.

It's no use arguing with a parent who's in this sort of state. The best thing is just to let him cool off[2]. But you might try to **distract** him and offer him a **graceful** way out by suggesting something that's fun to do, like **taking it out on** your little brother instead. [...]

BE FRIENDLY BUT FIRM. In general, don't give your parents too much chance to argue. Just quietly get on with whatever you want to do, perhaps chatting amiably[2] to distract their attention. The chances are they won't even notice, or that when they do it will be too late for them to feel like making a fuss.

Parents can sometimes drive a small child almost to distraction by **dawdling** about in shops, or talking to friends. It doesn't really help to keep nagging, or to try dragging them along by brute[2] force. If I were you I'd hop cheerfully about from foot to foot, and say in a firm, friendly voice: 'I want to go to the lavatory.' If that doesn't work, you could try turning white, and saying you're going to be sick.

REMEMBER YOU'RE HELPING THEM TO GROW UP. It's your job to help your parents grow up into mature responsible old-age pensioners[2], self-confident, armed with a workable code of morals and manners, and too exhausted in mind and body to make trouble for anyone else. If you keep in mind that you're training your children's grandparents you won't go far wrong.

→ **crayoning** ['kreɪənɪŋ] Read on – the meaning becomes clear at the end of the paragraph.
→ **inclined** Do you need to know this to understand the gist?
17 **deprived of** not having had
18 **lack of** absence of

→ **to handle** You often see "Fragile. Handle with care!" on parcels. This will help you guess the meaning.

26 **whim** sudden wish which is not the result of a strong purpose

39 **to distract s.o.** to stop s.o. concentrating on what they are doing
→ **graceful** Do you need to know this to understand the gist?
41 **to take it out on s.o.** to behave in an unpleasant way towards s.o. because you are angry or upset

48 **to dawdle** to spend more time than is necessary doing s.th.

From *The Original Michael Frayn* by Michael Frayn, London: Methuen Humour Classics, 1983, pp. 151–154.

Reading and thinking ▶

Parody
Speech, text or music that imitates and exaggerates the style of a well-known text in order to be amusing.

Hyperbole
A statement which is exaggerated for effect.

Understatement
Opp. of hyperbole; s.th. that is represented as being less important than it really is.

1. Did you enjoy the text? Why, why not?
2. According to "Spock's Guide", how should children treat their parents? List and explain his practical advice.
3. This text is a *parody* of books on childcare written by Dr Benjamin Spock, a world-famous American doctor. Look at the paragraph beginning "TEMPER TANTRUMS" (l. 31). What do you think the real Dr Spock would have written about young children and temper tantrums? Rewrite this paragraph.
4. Find examples of irony, *hyperbole* and *understatement* in the text. How do they support the effect of the parody?
5. What are the basic characteristics of a 'guide'? Use "Spock's Guide" as an example. You could refer to its contents, structure and function.
6. Imitating the author's style, write an additional paragraph on how teenagers should treat their parents. Use a conflict or a demand as a starting-point, for example pocket money, homework, household duties or the times you are expected home.

Close-up: vocabulary ▶

WB: p. 17, Vocabulary test

1. Which words from the text do you think it would be useful to learn? Write them down and add words from their word families. See page 120.
2. The class divides into 'teams'. Each team chooses five words or expressions from the text and writes a definition for each in English. The definitions are then read aloud to the other teams, who have to guess the correct phrase or word.

A step further ▶

WB: pp. 6–7, Grammar review

- Rewrite Spock's advice as a rap. You may use these lines to get started:

  If your parents get balky, just try to keep cool,
  'cause you're in command and shouldn't act the fool,
  put your drawings on the wall, then retire to bed,
  let them take it out on your brother instead!

  After practising speaking it rhythmically, present your rap to the class.
- You plan to put Spock's advice into practice. In groups, prepare a sketch (see page 117) in which his recommendations either fail or succeed. Act it out in class.

Describe the situation in the cartoon.
What might have happened during the days before?
Suggest a title for the cartoon.

Mildred

- a) Collect words which are used for the members of a family. Then draw your family tree and say how the members are related. Explain it to a partner.
  b) The relationship between the children in a family is not always marked by harmony, cooperation and love. According to your experience, what conflicts are typical signs of sibling rivalry (i.e. competition between brothers and sisters)? If you had a choice, what would be your 'dream/nightmare sibling constellation' (number, age, sex of siblings)? Give reasons.
- Write a *mini-saga* on sibling rivalry in which these five expressions appear: sister – goldfish – to pretend – perfectly normal – to slam the door.
- a) One of the characters in the story says: "I'm living the ultimate experience." Can you imagine what he/she is trying to express?
  b) What would your "ultimate experience" be?

Before you read

Mini-saga
A story of exactly 50 words.

▶ *When you read the following short story, try to work out the meaning of the words marked with numbers using the techniques described on page 108. To help you, they have been summarized on the right. Remember – you don't need to understand the meaning of every single word!*

Surviving without a dictionary
1 refers to *word family*
2 refers to *similar German, French or Latin words*
3 refers to *context*

WB: pp. 18–19, Understanding and learning new words

My name is Milly, which is short for Mildred, which is short for "Mil-dred". To my way of thinking *nobody* should be named Mildred except that my father's mother was and I guess he thought it was a good idea to name me after her. I never knew her, though, because she died before I was born. There's *another* name that's big in our family: Susan – which isn't terrific but is better than Mildred. Anyway, it's my maternal[2] grandmother's name ... my mother's name ... and of course my sister's name. Susan Marie Phelps. Susie. A name you can live with ... be proud of ... make proud of *you*. Which Susie hasn't exactly done. But that may be a prejudiced opinion.

Susie's always been a thorn[2] in my side, which my mother likes to believe is "perfectly normal sibling rivalry" except that I have friends who experience "perfectly normal sibling rivalry" almost daily and they don't have to put up with what I've put up with from Susie through the years.

Susie was thirteen when I was born and in some ways it was as though we were in two different families except that we had the same mother and father and both grew up in the same rambling house with the big wraparound front porch. One would think that having only one sister, and her that much older, would be sort of like being an only child except that even when Susie wasn't there, she was. I mean we could never stop thinking about her.

The one time I referred to her as a "bad seed", my mother cried and my father stared moodily out the window and the air in the room got heavy with unsaid things. Susie didn't do anything because as usual Susie was gone. Her "goneness" was a fact of life. Hers, mostly, but mine, too, because whatever Susie did seemed to spread over to me like milk spilled on a tabletop.

For example. The first birthday party I remember – the one where Amanda Shultz brought me the goldfish in the bowl – Susie was gone. I

14 **to put up with s.th.** to accept s.th. even though it might be unpleasant

17 **rambling** with many additions
17 **wraparound ... porch** *here:* veranda with a roof which goes around the whole house

22 **bad seed** black sheep in the family

Surviving without a dictionary

1 refers to *word family*
2 refers to *similar German, French or Latin words*
3 refers to *context*

know because Nana (Grandmother Susan) came over and ran the party while Mom and Dad huddled[3] upstairs next to the telephone, and then later on a policeman came and even a little kid knows that you can have a clown at a birthday party but never a policeman. Susie came back that time at Christmas and Mom and Dad pretended[3] nothing had happened and I got a pain in my stomach on account of their pretending so hard. She left another time the night of my piano recital[3] when I was the only one of Mrs. Cole's students to play "The Skater's Waltz" and I lost my place twice just looking at the door to see if my parents'd gotten there yet (and afterward they told me how good I was and tried to pretend they'd been there all along. And I let them.) Then there was my sixth birthday when she disappeared[1] between the time Mom left to take seven little girls to the movies and when we got back for cake and ice cream. And I'll never forget the year we were finally going to New England for our vacation and Susie turned up on the doorstep just as Dad and I were loading the car and we had to unload it and carry everything back inside and wait three days while Mom and Dad and Susie had long and heartfelt[1] talks.

We repeated this boomerang[2] pattern forever: Susie leaving, Susie coming back, and, in between, me leading some average everyday kind of life. It's not that Susie deliberately[3] set out to ruin[2] all the great occasions of my life – it just worked out that way. Anyhow, this isn't an exercise in feeling sorry for myself (the way Great-Aunt Hilda used to do and which we all found grossly[3] unattractive) but rather a statement of fact. And also to explain what happened later, along with what Nana refers to as my smart-aleck attitude toward life and what Mum calls my defense mechanism[2].

The last time Susie left, when she was twenty-three and I was ten (the day of my class trip to Mount Vernon, naturally, when Mom was supposed to chaperone but couldn't) Mom and Dad confronted[2] her at the breakfast table and said that enough was enough; that Susie was certainly old enough to be on her own; to live her life as she saw fit; that it was better, since she obviously couldn't live by their standards, that she live somewhere else; but that they'd always be there for her. I don't think any of us knew how there they were going to have to be. The thing is that when someone leaves the way Susie left (with her clothes in a plastic leaf bag thrown into the back of a friend's Volkswagen) and slamming the door behind her, she's sometimes more there than if she'd never left in the first place.

I mean it's hard to tell which were worse: the months when we didn't hear *anything*, or the frantic[3] phone calls, usually asking for money, that came late at night or early in the morning because Susie never managed to handle the difference in time zones[2]. In between there were occasional postcards or letters telling how she was experiencing life to the fullest; that she was into Zen, or est; was working as a waitress, a puppeteer[1], a ticket taker at a wildlife preserve[3], a deckhand[1] on a fishing boat. The letters themselves were short and somehow skimpy looking but Mom saved them all, storing[3] them away in the top drawer of the desk in the living room. Sometimes when no one else was home I'd take them out and reread them, as if trying to piece together my sister.

55 **smart-aleck** *(AE)* [smɑ:t 'ælɪk] too clever, as if one knows everything

59 **to chaperone s.o.** ['ʃæpərəʊn] to accompany s.o. and watch over them

61 **to do as one sees fit** to do what one thinks is right

73 **to be into s.th.** *(informal)* to be interested in s.th.

73 **Zen** Zen Buddhism

73 **est** = Erhard Seminars Training; alternative philosophy and technique intended to raise self-awareness

75 **skimpy** *here:* not very detailed

Then, even for Susie, she outdid herself. And I was the one who got the message[3]. On the answering machine.

Since Mom and Dad both work, I usually beat them home in the afternoon and the first thing I do (after getting something to eat) is to check the answering machine. I mean, even though I've just left practically[2] everyone I know at school, there's something about that glowing red light that makes me have to "rewind" and "replay". The weird thing was that with that particular message all set to uncurl[3] one would definitely think the red light would've given off an ominous[2] sort of glow. Which it didn't.

"Hi, Mom. Hi, Dad." The tape sounded garbled because it was worn[3] and nobody'd thought to get a new one. "I'm living the ultimate experience. I'm pregnant and I'm heading home. See you soon."

My first thought was to "erase[1]." My second was that there was no way I was going to give that message to my parents. And my third was to escape. So I rewound the tape, retraced[3] my steps out of the house, and headed[3] for the library, where I slumped[3] down in a chair and started into *Rebecca* for about the seventeenth time except that the whole time I was trying to read Susie's voice kept sounding inside my head: ... ultimate experience ... pregnant ... coming home. ...

I stayed at the library so long, I was afraid my parents would begin to worry, but when I got home I saw I needn't have bothered[3]. I mean, they were worrying, all right, but not about me. "Do you know what she's done now?" my mother said.

"Who's she?" I said. "Princess Di? Fergie?" My voice sounded wooden[1], the way thinking about Susie sometimes made me feel.

"Your sis-ter," said Mom.

I wanted to say, "I don't have a sister," but when I looked at my mother's face something pinched[3] inside of me like a too-tight shoe.

"What?" I said instead, turning away and trying to act like I didn't know what she was going to say next.

"She's pregnant."

"Pregnant?" The surprise in my voice sounded fake[3], but Mom didn't seem to notice.

"Don't say that word in front of the child," my father said. And since my father prides himself on being an open and forthright[3] kind of person (and since I'm fifteen and definitely not a child), that gives some idea how deep he was into denial.

"That's what she said," my mother went on. "Pregnant." And it was as if she had trouble getting her mouth around the shape of the word. "Maybe she's married. Maybe she just wants to surprise us."

"Mar-ried?" said my father, his voice cracking somewhere between the two r's. "Did she say anything about a husband? Did she say anything about a father? No, she did not. I'll tell you what she said – she said she was experiencing a – the –"

"She said she was living the ultimate experience," said Mom, going to stand by the window and looking out into the dark.

Susie came home by bus and walked up from the station with a canvas tote bag slung[3] on her shoulder. She looked pale and haggard[3] and older than the twenty-eight years I knew her to be. For a minute I almost felt

79 **to outdo o.s.** [-'-] to do even better than you have previously done
81 **to beat s.o. home** *(informal)* to get home before s.o.
85 **rewind** [aɪ] **rewound, rewound**
85 **weird** [wɪəd] strange
88 **garbled** confused
95 ***Rebecca*** romantic novel by the English writer Daphne du Maurier (1938)
113 **to pride o.s. on s.th.** to be proud of s.th.
115 **denial** [dɪ'naɪəl] *here:* refusal to admit
126 **pale** white
126 **haggard** ['hægəd]

Surviving without a dictionary

1 refers to *word family*
2 refers to *similar German, French or Latin words*
3 refers to *context*

131 **bear hug** putting one's arms around s.o. tightly to show love, affection

157 **to throw up** *(informal)* to be sick, to vomit

173 **to scrub s.th.** to rub s.th. hard to clean it

sorry for her – until I looked at my mother and father and they looked paler and even more haggard.

"Well, Susan," my father began. But whatever speech he had planned fizzled[3] out and after a minute he wrapped Susie in an enormous bear hug.

"Yes, well Susie," my mother began. "It's not the way we planned it – I mean the way we thought it would be," she said, dabbing[3] at her eyes.

"But that's just the point," the old Susie said, extricating[3] herself from my father's arms. "It's that way I planned it. I mean, I'm not getting any younger and I've always felt that giving birth is life's ultimate experience. And I want it all."

"But – but – but –" My father was fairly sputtering[3]. "What about the father?"

"What do you see as his role in all this?" my mother said.

"I don't see him as having a role. In fact, I plain don't see him at all anymore," my sister answered in a voice that clearly said that was all the explanation we were going to get.

And it was all the explanation we did get.

It was then that I entered my life-on-the-other-side-of-the-door phase[2]. The door was any door, with Mom, Dad, and Susie on one side and me crouched[3], head against the wood, on the other. I got used to hearing in phrases: "… stay here until …" "… up for adoption[2] …" "… best for the child …" "… sense of responsibility …"

And always, after a while, Susie shouting out, "I want this baby. I'm going to keep it."

Then there would be another door and another set of phrases: "… mother's raised her children …" "… a job, and day care …" "… here till you get on your feet[2] …" "… give you all the help we can but …"

And again, Susie: "… leave if you don't want me here …" "I've changed …" and "I want this baby."

The thing is, Susie did get a job (just as soon as she stopped throwing up). It was a job in an office and you could tell she didn't think it could compare to being a waitress, a puppeteer, a ticket taker at a wildlife preserve, or a deckhand on a fishing boat. And she didn't leave. Though the truth is that there were times, in the middle of the night, or even in Latin class, when I wished she would. I mean (and I have to say this in a whisper, even to myself) there were times when my sister Susie seemed more like a stranger than a stranger would have been.

"Is she going to *stay* here?" I asked my mother one night when we were doing the dishes.

"Of course she is," said Mom. "This is her home the same as it's yours."

"What about the kid? It won't even have a name."

"Of course it will," snapped Mom. "Its name will be Phelps."

"But that's *my* name," I heard myself whine[3] (just like Great-Aunt Hilda used to do).

"It's our *family* name," my mother said, scrubbing at the broiler pan. And then, after a minute, "Mil-dred, I'd hate to think you were embarrassed about your own sister."

Which is exactly what I was. I mean, there we were in the midst[1] of the sexual revolution and I was embarrassed[2]. Besides that, all of a sudden she was looking like Lucille Ball when she was pregnant on the *Lucy* show. She waddled. She lumbered[3]. And when my friends came over they'd all sneak[3] little glances at her from the side and then pretend not to notice.

It seemed like my whole family was into being what Mom called "supportive[1]." She bought Susie a new robe to take to the hospital, a bunch of baby clothes, and a stuffed bear. Dad got the old crib out of the attic and scrubbed it down. Nana made curtains for the nursery[3].

Correction: My whole family except me was into being supportive. When Susie and I were alone in a room together there still didn't seem to be anything to say, and the night she told me she was dying of boredom[1] and could we please go to the movies I told her I had a headache. And then hated the way I felt afterward.

When Susie went to childbirth[1] classes Mom went with her. A couple of times my mother tried to get me to go, saying that it would help me to be a part of things (which I definitely didn't want to be a part of), but I always managed to get out of it until one night after dinner when Mom tried again and I said no again and Dad said, "Mil-dred ... it would be a help to your mother," in that no-nonsense voice of his. And all of a sudden there I was in this big room with pregnant women all over the floor, along with husbands, significant others[3], and my mother. While Mom helped Susie breathe (helped her breathe?) I sat in the corner and tried to pretend I'd just stopped in[1] to get out of the rain. Which is what I did for all the rest of the classes, though I guess my mother didn't notice, because when they were finished Mom sighed a big sigh and said, "Well, now, I certainly feel better that there're two of us prepared to help Susie."

Prepared? To help her do what? I mean, I wasn't the one having a baby. In fact, I wasn't even sure I liked babies all that much.

And then Mom got a toothache. Not a little twingy run-of-the-mill toothache but a huge, throbbing[3] kind that needed a root canal and kept her up all night and sent her out to an emergency dentist appointment early the next morning.

"Wow," said Susie, waddling into the kitchen just as Dad and Mom pulled out of the driveway[1].

"Wow what?" I said, trying not to look at her standing there in her pink pajamas with the pants scooping down[3] under her enormous belly[3].

"Another one," said Susie.

"Another what?"

"Pain. Another pain," said Susie.

"What do you mean another pain?" I shrieked[3] at her. "Has there been one before?"

"All night," my sister said, turning a funny gray color and hanging on to the door frame.

"Why didn't you tell Mom? Call her," I said running to the kitchen window as if I thought the car might still be in the driveway[1]. "We'll call her at the dentist ... we'll –"

"No," said Susie. "There isn't time. And besides, she has to get that tooth taken care of. We'll take a taxi."

"A taxi?" I said. "We can't take a taxi. I only have a dollar."

178 **Lucille Ball** (1911–1989) actress, producer and comedienne
179 **to waddle** [ɒ] to walk with short steps swaying slightly from side to side (like a duck)
183 **crib** *(AE)* bed for a baby

205 **twingy** ['twɪndʒɪ] slightly painful
205 **run-of-the-mill** ordinary, normal

"In Mom's top dresser drawer," said Susie turning and heading for the stairs, walking as though she were stepping on eggs, and calling back over her shoulder, "There's money there. Mom told me. In case I was ever here alone and needed a cab."

In the hospital there were people who took information and blood and who examined[2] Susie to see how things were going and then said that they were going fine. And quickly. Then Susie and I were alone in a room together, except for the people coming in and out, and she rocked and sang and rested some. She groaned and grunted[3] and moaned[3]. She laughed a lot and showed me how to rub her back and when she looked tense[3] I told her to relax and when she said she couldn't stand it anymore I said she could and that she was.

Then it was as if everything went into fast forward[1] and there was someone handing me a funky green gown and all of a sudden we were in another room with bright lights and tile on the walls. A nurse told me to stay out of the way and if I felt faint[3] to sit down, but Susie called for me and I went to stand by her head. Her face was sweaty and twisted and smiling all at the same time and suddenly there was a thin watery cry as if from far away and someone plunked[3] this ugly, slimy[2], beautiful baby across Susie's chest and said, "It's a girl ... a girl ... a girl ..." in a voice that seemed to sing out loud.

I wiped[3] my sister's face and after she had looked at the baby all over she said, "We'll call Mom and Dad and tell them now. About the baby, and the name."

"Name?" I said, as if it were news to me that babies had them.

And then she said it. Susie, my sister, said that this baby – this niece – was going to be named Mildred.

For a minute I started to tell her that that was a rotten[3] thing to do to some unsuspecting kid. Then I caught myself[3]. I mean, I stood there looking at the baby with its funny spiky hair, stark naked[2] with its screwed-up face and its fists flailing, and thought how already she looked tough and precocious and incredibly smart, and definitely ready for the challenge. Because if there's one thing that makes life interesting it's the challenge.

If you don't believe it, ask Susie; ask me; or wait a few years and ask Mildred Marie Phelps.

234 **to rest some** *(AE)* to rest a little

239 **funky** *(slang)* modern, crazy
240 **tile** small flat square pieces used to cover a wall

242 **sweaty** [e] covered with small drops of liquid (because one is hot, frightened, etc.)

244 **slimy** [aɪ]

254 **unsuspecting** unknowing
256 **to flail** to hit about wildly
257 **precocious** [prɪˈkəʊʃəs] looking or behaving in a way that makes you seem older than you are

By Colby Rodowsky from *Connections,* New York: Dell Publishing, 1989, pp. 95–104.

Reading and reflecting ▶

1. a) What scenes from her childhood does Mildred describe? What have they got in common?
   b) Find phrases and sentences in the story that reveal Mildred's attitude to Susie. How does this attitude change in the course of the story?
   c) How do the parents feel about Susie's behaviour? Would you regard them as 'good parents'? Give reasons.
2. Sum up the *plot* of "Mildred" in not more than 100 words (see page 116).

Talking about how events are connected

At the beginning (of…)
Then/Later/Afterwards
Therefore/For this reason
As a result/Consequently
While/In the meantime…
Finally/In the end/At last
At the end of…

Plot

The plot of a story, novel or play is the sequence of events as arranged by the author. It says what happens, and why.

Suspense

Suspense is the feeling of expectation or excitement aroused in the reader by a well-constructed plot about what is going to happen.

3. "28-year-old Susie is a grown-up; Mildred, in contrast, is still a child when telling the story." Do you think this is true? Discuss in detail.
4. Read the *short story* box and apply the new terms to this short story.

Short story

A *short story* is a short fictional prose text which is meant to be read in a single sitting. It can be as short as 500 and as long as 15,000 words. A lot of stories follow different patterns but the following points apply to many of them:
- There may be one main character *(protagonist)* or a group of equally important characters.
- There is a *single setting* (i.e. the time and place of the action does not change). However, longer short stories might have more than one setting. The setting also helps to create a certain *atmosphere*.
- The reader may be led into the story through an *exposition* (the introduction of the main character(s), the theme and the setting). In modern stories the action often starts immediately in the first sentence.
- In some stories the action develops logically through conflicts or crises and finally reaches a *climax* or *turning-point* near or at the end (emphasis on action and suspense).
- Some stories concentrate on a decisive moment in the life of the main character (emphasis on character and psychology).
- There is often a *surprise ending*, a *happy/unhappy ending* or an *open ending*.

5. To what extent does a *first-person narrator* influence:
   a) the information you get?
   b) your attitude to, and sympathy for the characters?

First-person narrator

A first-person narrator ("I") is a character in the text who tells the reader what he/she thinks and feels. His/Her view of the events is always limited to what he/she knows and experiences (a limited point of view). The first-person narrator is not identical with the author.

A step further

- What would be Susie's view of the events described in the story? Rewrite the first part of the story (up to line 47) with Susie as first-person narrator.
- Choose one of the following two statements about the story:
  "At least she should have married the child's father."
  "I don't see the child's father as having a role."
  Collect arguments for the statement you have chosen. Then give a one-minute oral statement. See "How to give a talk" on page 107.
- What do you think will happen to the characters in the next ten years? Why?

WB: p. 8, Spoilsport; p. 21, Characters; p. 23, Guess what?

project

Following your suggestion, "Mildred" is going to be made into a film. Get into groups of three or four and prepare an attractive 'information pack' to market the film idea. See page 123 for further help.

Just for you!

A novel experience

Looking at literature

Before you read ▶

- Brainstorm for ideas in class and decide what features a novel should have to be enjoyable.
  a) Which features are more important than others? Rank your ideas according to their importance.
  b) Have you already read a full-length original novel in English? Can you recommend it as a class reader? Why, or why not?
- Before you read the following extracts look at the title and the cover of each book. What do you expect the book to be about?

Here are some techniques to help you guess the meaning of unknown words (also cf. page 108 for help):
– Look for members of a word family you already know.
– Think of similar German, French or Latin words.
– Does the context help you to understand the word?
– Does the way the word sounds give you an idea of what it means?

The following extracts from young-adult fiction and popular literature should help you and your classmates to choose a novel with a message but that is fun to read, too. You could work in groups, each group reads one extract.

"The court case" from *The Guilty Party* by Joan Lingard

Josie took the stand keeping her head up and her back straight. Rod shifted his head so that he could get a clear view of her. She appeared to be completely in control of herself and she looked so pretty, with her face flushed pink and her eyes sparkling. He knew there would be a sparkle in them even though he was not close enough to see it for himself.

The counsel for the defence said, "You have heard the two previous witnesses identify you as one of the people who lay down on the road. Do you deny that you did?"

"No, I do not."

"Can you explain to us why, if you admit that you did cause an obstruction, that you have pleaded not guilty?" Josie turned so that she half faced the court. This is the moment she had been waiting for, thought Rod. He leant forward in his seat.

"I pleaded not guilty because I do not believe that I have committed a crime against society. I lay down in the road as a gesture to show that I am opposed to this nuclear power station. I believe that the electricity board will commit a much more serious crime against society if it goes ahead. It could expose us to the possibility of an accident such as they had at Chernobyl."

The magistrate was growing restless; scratched his nose, cleared his throat, pursed his lips. Josie continued, speaking a little more quickly, "Thousands of people do not want this nuclear power station. We consider it to be unnecessary and we fear for the consequences if it is switched on. I believe, in a democracy, that the wishes of the people should be considered. We want another public enquiry. We deserve to have it. Things have changed, people have changed their minds – since Chernobyl!"

Some of the people in the public benches clapped and the clerk of the court said, "Silence in court!" and the magistrate frowned.

"Thank you, Miss McCullough," said the counsel for the defence and gave way to the prosecuting counsel who was on his feet to cross-examine the witness.

4 **to sparkle** to shine brightly
6 **counsel for the defence** *Verteidiger*
6 **previous** the one before this one
8 **to deny s.th.** [dɪ'naɪ] to say that s.th. is not true
11 **obstruction** blocking the way into s.th.
18 **to expose** *opp. of* to protect
20 **magistrate** an official who acts as a judge in the lower courts
21 **to purse one's lips** to form one's lips in a closed, round shape
25 **public enquiry** investigation by the authorities where the findings are made public
25 **to deserve s.th.** to have earned the right to s.th.
29 **to frown** to show in one's face that one is angry
31 **prosecuting counsel** *Vertreter der Anklage (Staatsanwalt)*

"You are obviously an intelligent young woman capable of both speaking and writing fluently," he began. He spoke smoothly. He smiled. Josie looked guarded. "You must be aware that there are ways of making your opinions known other than by lying in the road and causing an obstruction?"

"Well, yes, but –"

"Were you aware at the time that you were breaking the law when you lay down in the road?"

"Yes."

"That will be all, thank you."

Josie was instructed to stand down and was led back to the dock.

The counsel for the defence summed up briefly, saying: "My client acted out of genuine concern and not at all with the intention of making trouble. She is a young woman of high ideals who sincerely believes that nuclear power poses a real threat to the future of mankind and I would ask you to see her action in that light. Thank you."

The magistrate clasped his hands together on top of the bench and leaned forward. "You speak very eloquently, Miss McCullough, I congratulate you!" He bowed his head. "And I agree with you that the wishes of the people should be considered, but as my learned friend the counsel for the prosecution has indicated, there are other ways of making one's opinions known without resorting to lying in the road and breaking the law and causing a great deal of trouble for our police force which is overstretched as it is. If we were all to lie in the road to make our points the traffic would be brought to a complete standstill!" He paused. If he expected a titter of appreciation from the public benches he did not get it. "The fact remains that you have broken the law and so I have no alternative but to find you guilty." He broke off to turn to the police sergeant. "Is anything known about the defendant?"

"She has a previous conviction, sir, for obstruction."

The magistrate asked, "Would the defence counsel like to say anything about his client?"

"She is a young girl of limited means, sir. She is still at school."

"In that case I impose a fine of fifty pounds with the alternative of fourteen days imprisonment."

Josie lay on the bed in the courtroom cell, waiting. Waiting for something to happen. There would be a lot of waiting ahead, she fancied, and a lot of time to get through. All her possessions, including her books, had been removed from her. Why couldn't they have let her keep her books? What harm would it do if she were to read a novel by Alice Walker or a poem by Seamus Heaney? What was the point in stripping you of everything personal? Did they think that lying on a bare mattress staring at the ceiling would make you repent, see the error of your ways?

Suddenly, keys were rattling in the lock and the door was opening. A policewoman came in. "You're to be allowed to see your mother. So put on your shoes and come with me."

The Guilty Party by Joan Lingard, Stuttgart: Ernst Klett Verlag, 1992, pp. 105–108 and London: Penguin Books, 1989, pp. 113–116.

35 **to look guarded** not to show one's feelings
35 **to be aware of** to know about
44 **to sum up** to repeat all of the important points
45 **concern** worry
46 **sincerely** genuinely, truly
47 **to pose** *here:* to present
54 **to resort to s.th.** to turn to s.th. as the last possibility
58 **titter** nervous laugh
62 **conviction** [-'--] having been found guilty of a crime in court
66 **to impose a fine** to make s.o. pay a sum of money
69 **to fancy** to imagine
72 **Alice Walker** (b. 1944) African-American writer
73 **Seamus Heaney** (b. 1939) Northern Irish poet
75 **to repent** to be sorry for s.th. one has done

Chapter two

4 **hoarding** *(BE)* a large roadside sign
6 **to jabber** to talk senselessly
7 **to remove** to take away
9 **verge** [vɜːdʒ] strip of grass beside the pavement
9 **skinny** thin
25 **tadpole** baby frog
28 **Nab** Helen's horse
29 **to cling, clung, clung** to hold on tightly
35 **trolley** a small table on wheels
36 **syringe** [sɪˈrɪndʒ] device used to give injections
43 **to sob** to cry loudly taking in large amounts of air

"The abortion clinic" from *Dear Nobody* by Berlie Doherty

Helen is just about to begin her music studies when she finds out that she is pregnant. She tells her mother, who persuades her to have an abortion.

Dear Nobody,

It felt as if it was the last day of my life. Mum can't drive so I had to do it, and she never stopped talking. She kept reading out the street names as we passed them, and advertisements on hoardings, and even the registration numbers of the cars in front of us. It was as if she was frightened of silence. And all the time she was jabbering, I was forcing this into my head: this is simply an operation to remove unwanted cells from my body. That's all it is.

When I parked the car in the grounds of the hospital there was a dead bird on the grass verge, a tiny, skinny thing without feathers.

Mum sat with me while I was weighed and checked and then I had to change into a nightie. She put all my clothes into her bag. She was going to spend the night at her sister's, whose house was just down the road from the hospital. Auntie Pat would drive us back tomorrow. It was all carefully planned.

A doctor came in with a social worker and they sat and talked to me, and asked me if I was absolutely sure that this was what I wanted to do. My mouth didn't work properly. I wondered if they hated me. I wondered why they worked there. Then Mum held my hand and told me how brave I was being, and how I'd be able to go back to school at the end of the week and everything would be back to normal again. And then she couldn't bring herself to kiss me goodbye. I'd have put my arms round her if she had. I'd have asked her to stay with me because I was afraid.

The bed was high and the sheets were so stiff it was like lying between postcards. I lay on my side with my eyes closed and with my knees pulled right up to my chin and I tried to imagine what you looked like. You were twelve weeks old. You would be like a little pink tadpole. I'd looked you up in a medical book before we came. You would be about nine centimetres long. You weighed about fourteen grams.

I thought of myself on Nab's back, being thrown about like a doll, and I thought of you, a tiny thing, clinging on. You didn't think about anything and you didn't know anything and you clung on.

And when I was lying there, in all that silence, I felt as if it was me who was clinging on, as if you were my tiny self. I felt as if you knew something that I would never understand. And I felt as if I had become two people.

I was still trying to focus on you, trying to see through my fear to what it was that I was really frightened of, when the nurse came in with a trolley. She came too soon. I wasn't ready yet. She didn't speak to me. She held a syringe up to the light, and I felt hot and scared. I was just on the edge of panic then. I asked her what it was for and she told me I was going to have my operation.

I wanted Chris.

I told her I needed to talk to someone, and she told me to hold myself still, that it wouldn't take a minute, that it wouldn't hurt, that it would all be over soon. I could hear her voice; I could hear mine in my head but I couldn't make the words come out. I was sobbing out loud. I was pushing her arm away. She said if I needed to talk to someone she'd better get someone. As soon as she was out of the room I felt as if I could breathe again. I slid out of my bed and put my slippers on. There was nothing in my locker except my little tapestry shoulder-bag and my sponge bag and I picked them both up and went out. I thought at first that I was going to hide in the toilets but when I heard the nurse coming down the corridor talking to somebody I went straight past the toilets and found myself in the reception area. The receptionist had her back to me, looking for something in the filing cabinet and I walked straight past her and out through the doors into the car park. The keys were in my shoulder-bag and my hands were shaking but I managed to get the car open and to drive it out into the road. I once saw a film that started in black and white and then went into full colour. All of a sudden I noticed that the leaves on the trees were full green. People had scarlet tulips blazing away in their front gardens. When I pulled up at the traffic lights the woman in the car next to me glanced across and then said something to her passenger, and they both looked at me then and laughed. I don't blame them for laughing. I chuckled back at them. I liked that nightie, but I would have liked to tell them that usually I sleep in a long tee-shirt. No wonder I found it hard to drive; my slippers had bendy feet. I put a cassette on and wound down the windows and sang.

The worst bit came when I got home and had to walk over our pebbles in those bendy slippers.

I had a bath. I put a CD on really loud downstairs and left the bathroom door open. I hope you like music. [...]

I walked to Chris's school, taking a short cut through the park. It was full of young women with prams. I've never seen so many prams in my life before. The women all smiled at each other as they passed, as if there was some kind of conspiracy between them, as if they were members of a secret society.

Chris was one of the last to come out of the sixth-form block. He looked as if he'd been up all night. He was on his own, and he walked with his head down and his bags slung over his shoulder, as if he was miles away. He would have walked right past me if I hadn't called out to him. He went white when he saw me. I went up to him and waited for him to put his school-bag down, and when his arms were round me, I told him.

Little Nobody. I won't let go of you now.

* * *

"What do we do now?"

It was all I could think of asking, and when Helen said, "I don't know. You think of something," I suggested that we should run off to our cave on the Derbyshire moors. It was meant as a joke, really, to make her smile again.

"That's just your trouble, Chris." Her voice was tired and strained. She'd been through a hell of a lot that day. "You're too romantic. We've got to be practical about this."

"I've got twenty pounds," I said. "And a birthday coming up in August. I'll get a summer job."

There was nothing going round here, and I knew it. Most of the people on my street hadn't got jobs at all, at any time of the year, let alone in the summer. I'd have to go down south to get anything, and then where would I live?

"And after that?" said Helen, in a quiet voice. "When the baby's come? What do we do then, Chris?"

46 **slipper** soft shoe worn indoors
46 **locker** metal cupboard which can be locked
46 **tapestry** ['tæpɪstrɪ] heavy hand-woven cloth
47 **sponge bag** [spʌndʒ] *(BE)* bag for cosmetics, etc.
51 **filing cabinet** *Aktenschrank*
56 **scarlet** bright red
56 **to blaze** [eɪ] *(metaphor)* to shine brightly
59 **to chuckle** to laugh quietly
61 **bendy** soft, flexible
68 **pram** baby carriage
70 **conspiracy** [kən'spɪrəsɪ] secret plan

81 **Derbyshire** ['dɑ:bɪʃə]

83 **strained** *opp. of* relaxed; worried

88 **nothing going** no jobs available

Dear Nobody by Berlie Doherty, Stuttgart: Ernst Klett Verlag, 1998, pp. 69–73 and London: HarperCollins Publishers 1997, pp. 88–94.

Chapter two

"The dream-telling" from *The Giver* by Lois Lowry

Usually, at the morning ritual when the family members told their dreams, Jonas didn't contribute much. He rarely dreamed. [...]

But this morning was different. He had dreamed very vividly the night before.

His mind wandered while Lily, as usual, recounted a lengthy dream, this one a frightening one in which she had, against the rules, been riding her mother's bicycle and been caught by the Security Guards.

They all listened carefully and discussed with Lily the warning that the dream had given.

"Thank you for your dream, Lily." Jonas said the standard phrase automatically, and tried to pay better attention while his mother told of a dream fragment, a disquieting scene where she had been chastised for a rule infraction she didn't understand. Together they agreed that it probably resulted from her feelings when she had reluctantly dealt punishment to the citizen who had broken the major rules a second time.

Father said that he had had no dreams.

"Gabe?" Father asked, looking down at the basket where the newchild lay gurgling after his feeding, ready to be taken back to the Nurturing Center for the day.

They all laughed. Dream-telling began with Threes. If newchildren dreamed, no one knew. "Jonas?" Mother asked. They always asked, though they knew how rarely Jonas had a dream to tell.

"I did dream last night," Jonas told them. He shifted in his chair, frowning.

"Good," Father said. "Tell us."

"The details aren't clear, really," Jonas explained, trying to recreate the odd dream in his mind. "I think I was in the bathing room at the House of the Old."

"That's where you were yesterday," Father pointed out.

Jonas nodded. "But it wasn't really the same. There was a tub, in the dream. But only one. And the real bathing room has rows and rows of them. But the room in the dream was warm and damp. And I had taken off my tunic, but hadn't put on the smock, so my chest was bare. I was perspiring, because it was so warm. And Fiona was there, the way she was yesterday."

"Asher, too?" Mother asked.

Jonas shook his head. "No. It was only me and Fiona, alone in the room, standing beside the tub. She was laughing. But I wasn't. I was almost a little angry at her, in the dream, because she wasn't taking me seriously."

"Seriously about what?" Lily asked.

Jonas looked at his plate. For some reason that he didn't understand, he felt slightly embarrassed. "I think I was trying to convince her that she should get into the tub of water."

He paused. He knew he had to tell it all, that it was not only all right but necessary to tell *all* of a dream. So he forced himself to relate the part that made him uneasy.

12 **to chastise** [tʃæs'taɪz] to criticize strongly for doing s.th. wrong
13 **infraction** breaking
14 **reluctantly** unwillingly
14 **to deal** to give
19 **to nurture** ['nɜ:tʃə] to feed and take care of
24 **to frown** to draw one's eyebrows together as if one is in deep thought
30 **tub** [ʌ] bath
33 **tunic** loose-fitting, dress-like garment
33 **smock** long, loose shirt, usu. worn to protect one's clothes
46 **to relate** to tell
47 **uneasy** uncomfortable

"I wanted her to take off her clothes and get into the tub," he explained quickly. "I wanted to bathe her. I had the sponge in my hand. But she wouldn't. She kept laughing and saying no."

He looked up at his parents. "That's all," he said.

"Can you describe the strongest feeling in your dream, son?" Father asked.

Jonas thought about it. The details were murky and vague. But the feelings were clear, and flooded him again now as he thought. "The *wanting*," he said. "I knew that she wouldn't. And I think I knew that she *shouldn't*. But I wanted it so terribly. I could feel the wanting all through me."

"Thank you for your dream, Jonas," Mother said after a moment. She glanced at Father.

"Lily," Father said, "it's time to leave for school. Would you walk beside me this morning and keep an eye on the newchild's basket? We want to be certain he doesn't wiggle himself loose."

Jonas began to rise to collect his schoolbooks. He thought it surprising that they hadn't talked about his dream at length before the thank you. Perhaps they found it as confusing as he had.

"Wait, Jonas," Mother said gently. "I'll write an apology to your instructor so that you won't have to speak one for being late."

He sank back down into his chair, puzzled. He waved to Father and Lily as they left the dwelling, carrying Gabe in his basket. He watched while Mother tidied the remains of the morning meal and placed the tray by the front door for the Collection Crew.

Finally she sat down beside him at the table. "Jonas," she said with a smile, "the feeling you described as the wanting? It was your first Stirrings. Father and I have been expecting it to happen to you. It happens to everyone. It happened to Father when he was your age. And it happened to me. It will happen someday to Lily."

"And very often," Mother added, "it begins with a dream."

Stirrings. He had heard the word before. He remembered that there was a reference to the Stirrings in the Book of Rules, though he didn't remember what it said. And now and then the Speaker mentioned it. ATTENTION. A REMINDER THAT STIRRINGS MUST BE REPORTED IN ORDER FOR TREATMENT TO TAKE PLACE.

He had always ignored that announcement because he didn't understand it and it had never seemed to apply to him in any way. He ignored, as most citizens did, many of the commands and reminders read by the Speaker.

"Do I have to report it?" he asked his mother.

She laughed. "You did, in the dream-telling. That's enough."

"But what about the treatment? The Speaker says that treatment must take place." Jonas felt miserable. Just when the Ceremony was about to happen, his Ceremony of Twelve, would he have to go away someplace for treatment? Just because of a stupid dream?

But his mother laughed again in a reassuring, affectionate way. "No, no," she said. "It's just the pills. You're ready for the pills, that's all. That's the treatment for Stirrings."

49 **sponge** [spʌndʒ] elastic substance with holes in it *(Schwamm)*

54 **murky** unclear

63 **to wiggle** to move with small quick movements

65 **at length** for a long time

70 **dwelling** place where people live

85 **to apply to** to be relevant to

The Giver by Lois Lowry, Stuttgart: Ernst Klett Verlag, 1998, pp. 34–36 and New York: Bantam Doubleday Dell, 1994, pp. 34–38.

"The color game" from *The War Between the Classes* by Gloria D. Miklowitz

In this extract, Amy, an American of Japanese origin, finds out about a social experiment her class is to participate in. It is explained by the teacher, Mr. Otero.

I liked Mr. Otero. Most kids did. It was because he seemed so really excited about what he taught. And from what I heard, he cared about the students, because you'd often find him staying late to talk. He was kind of funny, too. I liked how he joked about his baldness, saying what didn't grow on top grew twice as thick at his chin. And he sure had a knack of keeping my interest in class; fifty minutes went by like ten.

"Today," he said, coming around to the front of his desk, "we're going to begin a great social experiment. For the next four weeks we'll be playing what I call the Color Game. In just four weeks we're going to change the world." Otero began writing on the board as he spoke, turning from time to time back to the class. "Imagine you're on a new planet where colors represent special status," he said. "Blue is the highest color. Blues are superior beings. Think of purity, of blue bloods, those with money, respect, and prestige. Blue children attend private schools and go to the best colleges. Their parents travel without worrying about cost; they live the good life in beautiful homes with maids and gardeners. And they intend to keep it that way." Otero stood aside so the class could read what he'd written on the board. I copied it into my notebook: Blue = upper class.

"Now, below the Blues are the Dark Greens. Like the upper middle class on earth. Dark Green people are often workaholics. They figure if they try a little harder they'll make it to the Blues. Dark Green children almost always finish college. They're expected by their parents to go into the family business or become important in their professions. They're aware of the colors below them, the Light Greens and Oranges. But they're too busy trying to keep what they have and do even better to consider lending these less fortunate colors a hand."

What is my family? I wondered uneasily. *Dark Green? No, not quite. Aspiring to be.* Adam, of course was a Blue.

"Now, below the Dark Greens you'll find the Light Greens. They are the most numerous in society – the bluecollar workers, the lower middle class. Light Greens don't have it easy. If they have a job and a decent place to live where crime isn't too terrible, they're grateful. Their kids may go to junior college; few graduate. Light Greens aspire to become Dark Greens, but many are happy just to keep their heads above water."

Otero chuckled with a kind of delighted satisfaction. "Finally we come to the Oranges. Now, there's a sad group. They're often out of work, on welfare, in trouble with the law, and no matter how hard they work, if indeed they can get jobs, they can barely make ends meet. Since welfare breeds welfare, you find second- and third-generation Oranges with big families and often no father figure around."

"Oranges would like a bigger piece ... in fact any piece ... of the planet's apple pie, but the way society operates, they may never get it."

4 **baldness** not having any hair on one's head
6 **knack** [næk] ability
16 **maid** woman servant
21 **to figure** *(AE informal)* to think
22 **to make it** *(informal)* to be successful
25 **to be aware of** to know about
27 **to lend s.o. a hand** to help s.o.
28 **uneasily** in a worried way
29 **to aspire to s.th.** to want very much to be s.th.
34 **junior college** *(AE)* an institution offering a two-year course which is the equivalent of the first two years of college or university
38 **on welfare** receiving help or money from the state
39 **barely** only just
39 **to make ends meet** to have enough money to live
40 **to breed, bred, bred** to produce, to create

He paused, then said, "Of course these are all the stereotypes of our class system."

Even though I'd written it down, I wasn't sure all the colors were sorted out in my head yet. Pretty soon Otero would have us selecting a color. What did I want to be? Certainly not an Orange or Light Green. No. Who'd want to have to struggle so hard to get along? It would be fine to be a Dark Green or Blue. They had respect and money to live well. That's what I wanted.

"I hope you've got all the colors straight," Otero said, "because now I'm going to explain the rules of etiquette on this unique planet." He toyed with a stick of chalk, then said, "We have a system of bowing in our new society. Oranges must always show their inferiority by bowing when they meet their superiors, all colors above them. Light Greens must bow to the Dark Greens and Blues. Dark Greens bow to the Blues. But the Blues, bless them, don't bow to anyone. Why should they? They're top dogs." He thought for a moment. "We have sex discrimination in our society, also, but we'll discuss that next time we meet. I wouldn't want to confuse you with too much at once. Especially you *Oranges*."

I laughed, along with everyone else. It was easy laughing when you weren't the one looked down on, and I had no thought that I could possibly become an Orange.

49 **to get along** to manage to live

53 **etiquette** ['etɪket] proper behaviour in society

54 **to bow** [baʊ] to bend one's head to show respect

58 **bless them** *(exclamation)* expressing one's liking of s.o.

The War Between the Classes by Gloria D. Miklowitz, Stuttgart: Ernst Klett Verlag, 1998, pp. 25–27 and New York: Bantam Doubleday Bell, 1986, pp. 27–30.

Reading and comparing

1. What are your first impressions of the book based on the extract?
2. What image of young adults emerges from these pages? Do you feel represented? Do you think this image is biased, one-sided, dated...?
3. To what extent do particular elements in the extracts remind you of people you know or the world you live in?

Making a decision

1. Based on the extracts you have read, give a short talk (cf. p. 107) saying why you would, or would not, like to read the rest of the novel in class. Say what features are fascinating or uninteresting.
2. If you are still undecided, read the books in groups of two or three. Then, present them to the class. After that, pick one book to read as a class.
3. If none of the extracts or novels appeals to you, give a short talk (cf. p. 107) in which you present a novel you would prefer for class reading.

Understanding the novel

- While you read your chosen novel, keep a reading journal (cf. p. 110). Write down important insights into setting, characters, point of view, atmosphere, plot development, etc. When you have finished, exchange journals within a small group and discuss your findings.
- To better understand the novel, you could draw a mood chart (cf. page 111) or geographical map showing where key events happen (cf. page 110).

project

- Write a review of the book you have read. See page 108 for help.
- Write a letter to the publisher of the novel or to the author.
- Write a film scene for certain scenes in the novel (cf. pages 123).
- Write additional chapters where you think they might fit into the plot.
- Introduce yourself into the book and have a conversation with the protagonist and/or antagonist.

Focus on film

Films and actors

- In pairs, try to agree on five qualities which you think a successful film should have.
- a) Think of teenage characters you have seen in films. Does Leonardo DiCaprio's statement on the left apply to them, or not?
  b) To what extent can you identify with these characters? What qualities should your "hero" have?
- In groups of three or four, create and market your own film idea. Refer to the box "Talking about films" for useful vocabulary.
  – Draw up a list of four to six characters giving roles to as many of your favourite actors/actresses as possible. Then visualize the relationships between the characters on a poster/transparency. See page 15 for ideas.
  – Outline an interesting plot.
  – Present your ideas (cast and plot) to the class. Explain why you think your film idea could be commercially successful. See page 123 for help.
- a) Compare the three film posters below. In what ways are they similar or different?

  b) Which of the three posters appeals to you most? Why?
  c) Make your own poster for one of the film ideas developed in task 3, using ideas from the three posters above. Before you start you may want to consider these questions:
  – What is the function of a film poster?
  – What features should it have?
  – In what way is it to appeal to the various target groups?
- a) Think of a film you would recommend for an English film night in your school. Note down some reasons to support your suggestion.
  b) In a one-minute talk, give your arguments for the film you favour. Order your ideas in a convincing way, including some of the points in the box "Talking about films". See page 107 for help. Do not give the ending away!

"People want you to be a crazy, out-of-control teen brat. They want you miserable, just like them. They don't want heroes."

Leonardo DiCaprio, actor

Talking about films

cast (all the actors in a film)
the leading man/lady
a supporting actor/actress
to play a leading role
to play the part of … in …
a bit part (a very small role with few lines)
an extra (an actor with no lines, e.g. in a crowd)
to shoot a film:
  on set (in a studio)
  on location (in authentic surroundings)
prop (an object used on set)

You could mention:
the impression the film made on you – the plot (beginning, key scenes, the high point) – the build-up of suspense – the performance given by the actors/actresses – any special effects

Filmmaking – who does what?

- a) As a teenager, Stephen Spielberg charged admission to his homemade films while his sister sold popcorn. In your opinion, what qualities which he probably had as a teenager later made him a successful director/producer?

  b) Use the Internet to:
  – find out the plot of *Schindler's List.*
  – make a list of the films directed/produced by Stephen Spielberg and the topics they cover. Then, try to name the kind of film or 'genre' in each case. See the box below for help.

Film genres

an action film • an adventure film • a comedy • a drama • a fantasy film • a horror film • a mystery • a romance • a science-fiction film • a (crime) thriller • a Western

Stephen Spielberg is one of the most successful directors/producers in Hollywood's history. In 1993 he won Best Director and Best Picture Oscars with *Schindler's List*.

- a) Read the information in the box below. Who would you regard as the key figures in the making of a commercially successful film?

Filmmaking – who does what?

– The *scriptwriter* writes the *screenplay*, a 'play' for the 'screen', which only contains characters, action and dialogues. The screenplay is often based on a novel, a stageplay or a historical event.
– The *director/filmmaker* turns the screenplay into a *shooting script*, i.e. he/she makes changes to the screenplay and adds instructions for the actors and camera crew. The filmmaker controls and directs everything on the film set. He/she decides how to shoot each scene and is responsible for the film's creative development.
– An *editor's* job is to cut all of the film shot by the director into a final version.
– *Producers* look after the business side of making a film. First, they find the money and a film studio for a project. Then they manage the budget while the film is being made. Finally, they are in charge of marketing the film.

b) What practical decisions is a director faced with when making a film?
c) Which aspects of the director's role do Jodie Foster and Tom Hanks emphasize in the following quotes?

"As an actor, you have to sit in your trailer and be moody and mysterious and not come out till they need you. But the filmmaker has to communicate to everybody – and it doesn't start on the first day of shooting."

Tom Hanks, actor

"It would be great to be a director. They get to do anything (they like). They have people killed, blow things up, make people cry and laugh. Directing is just like creating life."

Jodie Foster, actress

d) Could you imagine doing a job in filmmaking, or not? If so, which of your interests, experiences and skills could you draw upon? See the box "Filmmaking – who does what?" for help.

In *The Phantom Menace* Jar Jar Binks is a talking, feeling, running, falling, fainting, amphibious, entirely computer-generated, comic relief character.

A computer-generated view of the Jedi Temple from *The Phantom Menace*.

"The effects budget on 'Titanic' was 40 million dollars and it accounts for about a half hour of the film. In 'Titanic', visual effects were extremely important in creating its key scenes. But of much greater importance was the love story and capturing the intimacy of those moments."

James Cameron, *Titanic* director

- a) What do you think of James Cameron's and George Lucas's remarks on digital filmmaking?

"On this movie [...] I could create shots and scenes in the editing room, rather than just cut them. I could move things around, cut people out of one shot and change locations. I could completely reconstruct and rewrite the story in the editing process."

George Lucas, *Star Wars* director

b) Look at the pictures from the film *The Phantom Menace* above. What possible advantages could a director have from computer-generated imaging? Refer to the box on "Computer-generated imaging" for ideas.

Computer-generated imaging

New computer programmes have made it possible to create realistic three-dimensional images: in this way, artificial figures become convincing characters, a variety of special effects can be included, images can be improved and complete locations created. Digital technology can save a lot in construction and travel costs.

c) Try to think of more examples of films which either include computer-generated imaging or are fully computer-made.

- "In the future, most films will be made using computers. Perfectly designed computer actors will take the place of real actors and actresses." How would you feel about films where this was the case?

Visualizing a film beginning

The following text, based on a filmmaker's manual, gives different versions of a film storyboard *(see definition below). As you read the text make a list of any words or phrases referring to the use of the camera. Use a dictionary to check any unknown words.*

◀ While reading

A filmmaker has chosen a suburban neighbourhood as the location for the opening scene of a film based on his childhood experiences. The opening scene describes a weekday morning when, as usual, he was the last member of the family to wake up.

Version 1 The filmmaker decides to limit himself to static shots using limited camera movement to follow the action. He begins with a long eye-level shot of the house. After a few moments the father goes out the front door and walks to the garage; the camera pans right to follow him. A new shot shows the window of the boy's bedroom through which we can see a corner of the bed as the father passes by outside. In shot 3, the camera zooms into a closeup of the boy's face...

Version 2 The improved version begins with a high-angle establishing shot which includes the house but also more surrounding space. A medium shot follows the father as he leaves the house. Then, a tracking shot shows him walking to the garage where he finds a running shoe in the grass. He picks it up. We cut to the next frame: shaking his head he walks a few steps towards the camera and sighs. Shot three is a low-angle one: the boy turns over in bed and his bare foot pops out from under the covers. We hear a door open, his father's hand enters the frame and puts the shoe on the bedpost...

Version 3 The film starts with an opening shot (extreme closeup) of a bright orange spaceship shaking in the morning breeze. The camera zooms out and we realize that we are looking at a torn kite in the high branches of a tree. The wind moves the kite which drops out of frame showing the house below. Cut to the boy in bed. Through the window we see the father backing the car out of the driveway. A squeal of brakes is heard. Cut to a low-angle shot of the driveway and the car, which has stopped a few feet from a running shoe in the foreground. The car door opens and the camera zooms out slightly to include the father's feet getting out of the car, then slowly tilts up to show his surprised face. The mother appears in the background, standing in the door frame. An over-the-shoulder shot shows the situation from her point of view...

Storyboard

A film director usually works with illustrators who visualize key scenes from the screenplay in a sequence of pencil drawings. The sketches may include arrows and give the cameraman an idea of the size of a shot and the camera movement. A board with these pictures (*storyboard*) is the basis for the shooting.

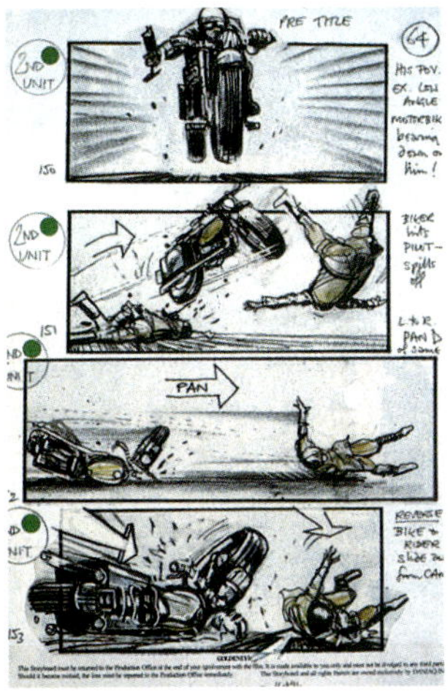

A storyboard for a scene from the film *Goldeneye*.

◀ Reading and thinking

1. Which of the phrases that you have found in the text refer to:
   – the size of the picture?
   – the angle, position or movement of the camera?
   See also the box "Camera operations" on page 112 and add any extra phrases to your list.
2. a) What do you like about Version 1? What do you not like about it?
   b) What exactly has been changed from Version 1 to Version 2, and again from Version 2 to Version 3?
   c) What could have been the reasons for these changes?

3. After the third version of the film opening, the filmmaker stops to rethink his latest version. He has generated some ideas but sees that they need to be rearranged. One new idea is to let the car bumper somehow catch the kite string and pull it along. To break the focus on the shoe action, he considers including more of the other family members. In addition, he would like to show that the father – like his son – is far from being perfect…
   a) Write the shooting script for the storyboard below. Focus only on setting, characters, dialogue and camera operations. See page 114 for help in writing your shooting script.
   b) In groups, share and discuss your ideas. Then, in the role of the director, one person introduces the film beginning to the class as if they were the actors, camera crew, etc. working on the set. The class can express an opinion and/or ask for further information.

Version 4

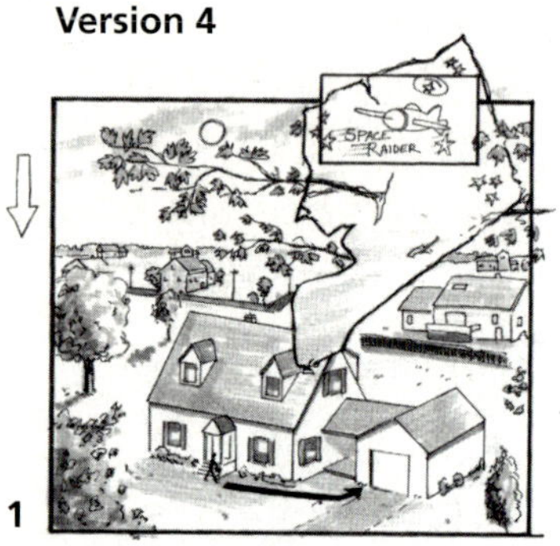

1

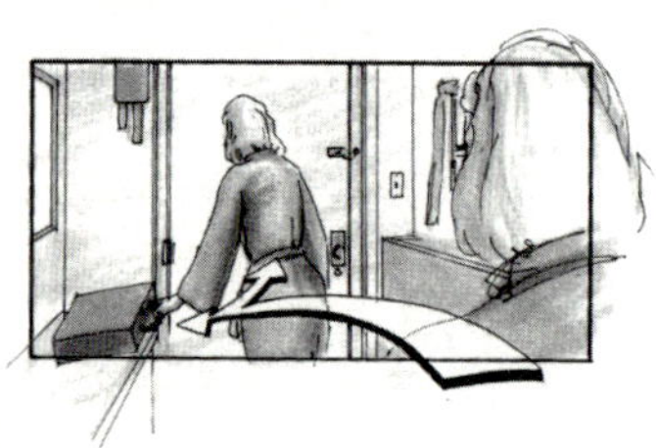
2

3

4

5

6

7

sound effects: sound of the car braking suddenly outside

8

9

sound effects: doorbell

10

11

12

Good Will Hunting – a scene in a bar

Before you read

- a) What do you know/remember about the plot and characters in the film *Good Will Hunting*?
  b) What kind of person does the protagonist Will Hunting (the young man in the picture on the right) seem to be?
  c) What impression do you get of the relationship between the two men?
- Four of the main roles in *Good Will Hunting* include a mathematics professor, a caring psychiatrist, the young girl Will falls in love with and a snobbish student from an elite university. As the casting director, choose your ideal cast for these four roles. Give reasons for your choice.

In 1997, the film *Good Will Hunting* was awarded an Oscar for Best Supporting Actor (Robin Williams) and Best Screenplay Written Directly For The Screen (Matt Damon and Ben Affleck). It was also nominated for seven more Oscars. Will Hunting (Matt Damon) is a university janitor whose talent for mathematics is discovered by a professor; a psychiatrist tries to help him with his talent and his life.

Setting: A crowded student bar.
Characters: Will Hunting, 20, handsome, confident, mathematical genius; Chuckie Sullivan, 20, loud, lively; Billy McBride, 22, heavy, quiet; Morgan O'Mally, 19, the smallest, thin but muscular. All four boys speak with thick Boston accents; they all come from a rough, working-class neighbourhood in Boston.

• Int. Bow and Arrow
Chuckie is collecting money from the guys to buy a pitcher. All but Morgan cough up some crumpled dollars.
CHUCKIE So this is a Harvard bar, huh? I thought there'd be equations and shit on the wall.

• Int. back section, Bow and Arrow – moments later
Chuckie returns to a table where Will, Morgan and Billy have made themselves comfortable. He spots two attractive Harvard women sitting together at the end of the bar. Chuckie struts his way toward the women and pulls up a stool. He flashes a smile and tries to submerge his thick Boston accent.
CHUCKIE Hey, how's it goin'?
LYDIA Fine.
SKYLAR Okay.
CHUCKIE So, you ladies, ah, go to school here?
LYDIA Yes.
CHUCKIE Yeah, 'cause I think I had a class with you.
At this point, several interested parties materialize. Morgan, Billy and Will try, as inconspicuously as possible, to situate themselves within listening distance. A rather large student in a Harvard lacrosse sweatshirt, CLARK, twenty-two, notices Chuckie. He walks over to Skylar and Lydia, nobly hovering over them as protector. This gets Will, Morgan and Billy's attention.
SKYLAR What class?
CHUCKIE Ah, history I think.
SKYLAR Oh…
CHUCKIE Yah, it's not a bad school…
At this point, Clark can't resist and steps in.
CLARK What class did you say that was?

1 **int.** *short for* interior, *here:* inside a building
1 **Bow and Arrow** name of a bar
2 **pitcher** container which holds liquid, e.g. beer
3 **to cough up** *(informal)* to give money unwillingly
4 **Harvard** elite university in Cambridge, near Boston
4 **equation** [ɪ'kweɪʒn] in mathematics, a statement that two amounts are equal
5 **shit** *(slang) here:* things like that
9 **to strut** to walk in an upright, proud way
10 **to submerge** *here:* to hide
19 **inconspicuously** not wanting to be noticed
20 **lacrosse** game played with a ball and sticks with nets on the end
22 **nobly** in a gentlemanlike way
22 **to hover** [ɒ] *here:* to stand in one place

CHUCKIE History.

CLARK How'd you like that course?

CHUCKIE Good, it was all right.

CLARK History? Just "history"? It must have been a survey course, then.

Chuckie nods. Clark notices Chuckie's clothes. Will and Billy exchange a look and move subtly closer.

CLARK Pretty broad. History of the world?

CHUCKIE Hey, come on pal, we're in classes all day. *(beat)* That's one thing about Harvard never seizes to amaze me, everybody's talkin' about school all the time.

CLARK Hey, I'm the last guy to want to talk about school at the bar. But as long as you're here I want to "seize" the opportunity to ask you a question.

Billy shifts his beer into his left hand. Will and Morgan see this. Morgan rolls his eyes as if to say, "Not again..."

CLARK Oh, I'm sure you covered it in your history class. *Clark looks to see if the girls are impressed. They are not. When Clark looks back to Chuckie, Skylar turns to Lydia and rolls her eyes. They laugh. Will sees this and smiles.*

CHUCKIE To tell you the truth, I wasn't there much. The class was rather elementary.

CLARK Elementary? Oh, I don't doubt that it was. I remember the class – it was just between recess and lunch.

Will and Billy come forward, stand behind Chuckie.

CHUCKIE All right, are we gonna have a problem?

CLARK There's no problem. I was just hoping you could give me some insight into the evolution of the market economy in the early colonies. My contention is that prior to the Revolutionary War, the economic modalities, especially of the southern colonies, could most aptly be characterized as agrarian precapitalist and...

Will, who at this point has migrated to Chuckie's side and is completely fed up, includes himself in the conversation.

WILL Of course that's your contention. You're a first-year grad student. You just finished reading some Marxian historian, Pete Garrison prob'ly, and so naturally that's what you believe until next month when you get to James Lemon and get convinced that Virginia and Pennsylvania were strongly entrepreneurial and capitalist back in seventeen forty. That'll last until sometime in your second year, then you'll be in here regurgitating Gordon Wood about the prerevolutionary utopia and the capital-forming effects of military mobilization.

CLARK *(taken aback)* Well, as a matter of fact, I won't, because Wood drastically underestimates the impact of –

WILL – Wood drastically underestimates the impact of social distinctions predicated upon wealth, especially inherited wealth. ... You got that from Vickers's *Work in Essex County*, was it pages ninety-eight to one-oh-two, what? Do you have any thoughts of your own on the subject or were you just gonna plagiarize the whole book for me?

Clark is stunned.

33 **survey course** general introductory course

36 **subtly** ['sʌtlɪ] not easily noticed

38 **pal** *(informal)* unfriendly address for a man

38 **beat** short pause

→ **to seize ≠ to cease** Look in your dictionary to find out what Chuckie could have meant.

→ **to seize** How does Clark try to make Chuckie look stupid?

53 **recess** [-'-] break between classes

→ Characterize Clark's speech in ll. 56–60. What is he trying to do?

58 **contention** *(formal)* opinion, argument

59 **modality** condition

59 **most aptly** best

61 **to migrate** *here:* to move

63 **grad(uate) student** student with a first degree who is doing further studies (a master's degree)

67 **entrepreneurial** [ˌɒntrəprə'nɜːrɪəl] business-oriented

68 **to regurgitate** [rɪ'gɜːdʒɪteɪt] *here:* to repeat

71 **taken aback** very surprised

72 **impact** effect

74 **predicated upon** *(formal)* based on

77 **to plagiarize** ['pleɪdʒəraɪz] to copy other people's ideas

78 **stunned** speechless

WILL Look, don't try to pass yourself off as some kind of an intellect at the expense of my friend just to impress these girls.

Clark is lost now, searching for a graceful exit, any exit.

WILL The sad thing is, in about fifty years you might start doin' some thinkin' on your own and by then you'll realize there are only two certainties in life.

CLARK Yeah? What're those?

WILL One, don't do that. Two, you dropped a hundred and fifty grand on an education you coulda picked up for a dollar fifty in late charges at the public library.

Will catches Skylar's eye.

CLARK But I will have a degree, and you'll be serving my kids fries at a drive-through on our way to a skiing trip.

WILL *(smiles)* Maybe. But at least I won't be unoriginal. *(beat)* And if you got a problem with that, I guess we can step outside and deal with it that way.

Although Will is substantially smaller, Clark decides not to take Will up on his offer.

WILL If you change your mind, I'll be over by the bar.

He turns and walks away. Chuckie follows, throwing Clark a look. Morgan turns to a nearby girl.

MORGAN My boy's wicked smart.

79 **to pass o.s. off as s.th.** to pretend to be s.th.
86 **to drop** *here:* to waste
86 **grand** *(AE informal)* a thousand dollars
87 **coulda** *(informal)* could have
87 **late charges** money you must pay when you return a book late
100 **wicked** *(informal) here:* terribly

From *Good Will Hunting – A Screenplay* by Matt Damon & Ben Affleck, New York: Hyperion, 1997, pp. 23–27.

◀ Reading and thinking

1. Briefly sum up the scene (setting, characters, action).
2. Divide the scene into parts and give a heading to each section.
3. Take a closer look at the characters and try to answer these questions:
   - Who is the main character in the scene? Why?
   - What is at stake for the protagonist?
   - What is the conflict in this scene?
   - How, if at all, does the protagonist change as a result of the conflict?
   - Is there a winner or loser in this scene?
4. As the scene progresses, how do your feelings towards the characters change? See the box on "audience empathy" below for help.

WB: p. 53

Audience empathy

Audience empathy is the viewer's ability to understand a film character's feelings as if they were his/her own. A filmmaker usually gets the audience to love the *protagonist* and hate the *antagonist*.

Audience empathy should be created as early as possible. To achieve emotional identification, the protagonist is often shown in crisis situations where he/she suffers from danger, loneliness, unkindness, humiliation or insecurity. In general, the characters in popular films are larger than life, yet still emotionally accessible to the audience. If a spectator identifies with a protagonist's struggles and ambitions, he/she will follow the story with greater interest.

5. Is the scene cinematic, i.e. is it visually attractive and with non-redundant dialogue? Give examples to support your answer.
6. To what extent can exercises 1 to 5 above be used to analyse any film scene? Develop your own checklist for film scene analysis.

Screenplay into shooting script ▶

1. Turn the scene script on pp. 41–43 into a shooting script (first draft). Make notes for each shot in a grid like the one below. See the box "Talking about camera operations" for help.

no. of shot	setting/characters/ action	dialogue	camera operations

Talking about camera operations

shot (uninterrupted sequence of pictures)
cut (switch from one shot to the next)
size of people/field size: long shot (people from a distance); full shot (shot of the whole body); medium shot (upper body); closeup (head and shoulders); extreme closeup (face only)
special camera positions: establishing shot (location of the scene); point-of-view shot (through a character's eyes); over-the-shoulder shot
camera angles: high-angle shot (from above); eye-level shot; low-angle shot (from below)
camera movements: static shot (no movement); to zoom in/out/into a face; to pan left/right; to tilt up/down; tracking shot (camera follows a vehicle moving on the ground)

2. In groups of six, act out the dialogue in the bar. How does the tone of the conversation change?
3. a) Divide the class into two groups. Then give everybody a role (actors, the director, the scriptwriter, the cameraperson). Rehearse the scene step by step. Give constructive feedback on body language, movements and language use. During the rehearsal correct and add to your first draft of the shooting script until you come up with a final version.
   b) Video the scene based on the final version of your shooting script. To set the scene, bring along suitable 'bar' props and music.
   c) Compare the versions produced by the two groups. Before you start, agree on the criteria necessary to produce "cinematic quality".

A step further ▶

- Compare the screenplay of the bar scene with the original film scene:
  – Have details been added or taken away? Has the scene been simplified or some point been given more/less importance?
  – Describe the use of the camera in terms of angle/position/movement and the size of the shots. Cf. the box on camera operations above for help.
- Compare your film versions with the original film scene.
- a) In the still on the left Will has just left the bar when he notices Clark inside. He approaches the window. What do you think Will says to Clark? What could be written on the note he is pressing to the glass?
  b) What do you think has happened since the conflict between Clark and Chuckie/Will? Write a scene script for the missing part, then compare your version with the corresponding part of the film.

A film critic voices his verdict

Before you read

- a) Do you usually read reviews of new films, or not?
  b) To what extent do film reviews influence your decision to see a film in the cinema?

Roger Ebert is one of America's most prominent film critics. He has published reviews in the Chicago Sun-Times *since the 1980s, including one of* Good Will Hunting *(an extract is given below). You can search his review archive on the Internet.*

It must be heartbreaking to be able to appreciate true genius and yet fall just short of it yourself. A man can spend his entire life studying to be a mathematician – and yet watch helplessly while a high school dropout, a janitor, scribbles down the answers to questions the professor is baffled by.

It's also heartbreaking when genius won't recognize itself, and that's the most baffling problem of all in *Good Will Hunting*, the smart, involving story of a working-class kid from Boston.

The film stars Matt Damon as a janitor at MIT who likes to party and hang around the old neighborhood and whose reading consists of downloading the contents of whole libraries into his photographic memory. Stellan Skarsgard plays Lambeau, the professor, who offers a prize to any student who can solve a difficult problem. The next morning, the answer is written on a blackboard standing in the hall.

Who claims credit? None of the students does. A few days later, Lambeau catches Will Hunting (Damon) at the board and realizes he's the author – a natural mathematical genius who can intuitively see through the thorniest problems. Lambeau wants to help Will, to get him into school, maybe, or collaborate with him. But before that can take place, Will and some buddies are cruising the old neighborhood and beat up a guy. Will also hammers on the cops a little and is jailed.

He's a tough nut. He sees nothing wrong with spending his whole life hanging out with his friends, quaffing a few beers, holding down a blue-collar job. He sees romance in being an honest bricklayer, but none in being a professor of mathematics – maybe because bricklaying is work, and, for him, math isn't. [...]

Good Will Hunting is the story of how this kid's life edges toward self-destruction and how four people try to haul him back. One is Lambeau, who gets probation for Will with a promise that he'll find him help and counseling. One is Sean McGuire (Robin Williams), Lambeau's college roommate, now a community college professor who has messed up his own life, but is a gifted counselor. One is Skylar (Minnie Driver), a British student at Harvard, who falls in love with Will and tries to help him. And one is Chuckie (Ben Affleck), Will's friend since childhood, who tells him: "You're sitting on a winning lottery ticket. It would be an insult to us if you're still around here in 20 years." [...]

Good Will Hunting has been rather inexplicably compared to *Rain Man*, although *Rain Man* was about an autistic character who cannot

1 **to appreciate** [ə'pri:ʃɪeɪt] to admire and understand
4 **janitor** ['dʒænɪtə] (*BE* **caretaker**) s.o. who looks after a building
5 **baffled** unable to understand
8 **involving** moving, emotionally touching
9 **MIT** Massachusetts Institute of Technology; elite technical university in Cambridge, Massachusetts
15 **to claim credit** *here:* to say that he has found the answer
18 **thorny** difficult (**thorn** = *Dorn*)
19 **to collaborate with** to work with
20 **to cruise** [kru:z] to drive slowly with no special destination
23 **to quaff s.th.** *(lit.)* to drink a lot of s.th. quickly
27 **to edge** to move slowly
28 **to haul** to pull with force
29 **probation** system by which a person guilty of a crime has to report to an official rather than going to prison *(Bewährung)*
30 **counseling** professional help with one's problems
31 **community college** *(US)* two-year junior college
37 **inexplicably** for unknown reasons
38 **autistic** [ɔ:'--] mental condition which prevents s.o. communicating with others

and does not change, and *Good Will Hunting* is about a genius who can change, and grow, if he chooses to.

Here is a character who has four friends who love and want to help him, and he's threatened by their help because it means abandoning all of his old, sick, dysfunctional defense mechanisms. As Louis Armstrong once said, "There's some folks, that, if they don't know, you can't tell 'em." This movie is about whether Will is one of those folks.

43 **dysfunctional** psychologically damaged

First published in the *Chicago-Sun Times*.

Reading and understanding ▶

1. A classmate suggests *Good Will Hunting* for an English film evening in your school. Basing your answer on the film review you have just read, how would you respond?
2. a) What do you learn about the characters and the plot of the film? Which particular film scenes are mentioned?
   b) Write down some questions about the film which are *not* answered in the review.
3. a) Find examples of where the reviewer gives his personal opinion.
   b) Critics often explicitly voice, or sum up, their opinion in a concluding paragraph, give the film a rating (e.g. on a scale of 0 to 10) or comment on the target audience. Add a paragraph to the Ebert review which includes these points.

A step further ▶

- a) Search the Internet for the Ebert review of a film you know very well. To what extent do you agree/disagree with Ebert's analysis?
  b) In class, think of one blockbuster which everybody has seen. Then search the Internet for different reviews of the film and compare them. Refer to the box below on "Talking about films and reviews" for useful vocabulary.

Talking about films and reviews

box-office hit/success • blockbuster • cult film/movie *(AE)*
box-office flop/failure • a top-grossing film
to gross 200 million dollars • to attract a target audience
a film stars/features an actor • viewers/filmgoers

critic • to write a review • to review a film
to meet with bad/unflattering/mixed reviews
to receive favourable/ecstatic reviews

WB: page 54

- Write your own short review of a film which is currently on show in the cinema. Give your opinion as to whether it is going to be a blockbuster or a box-office flop.
- Which aspects of "*Good Will Hunting* – a scene in a bar" (pp. 41–43) are referred to in the Ebert review?

The Graduate – from novel to film

After his graduation from college, Benjamin Braddock flies home to his parents. Some days after his arrival he turns twenty-one and gets a surprise birthday present from his parents: a rubber diving suit complete with a mask, oxygen tanks, flippers and a spear. Unwillingly, Ben puts on the diving gear in the house while the party guests, the Lewises and the Arnolds, wait outside for a demonstration in the swimming-pool.

Novel extract

Benjamin stepped out the door and into the back yard. The neighbors continued to clap and laugh. Sir Lewis pulled a handkerchief out of his pocket to dry his eyes. The Arnold children began jumping up and down on the lawn and screaming and pointing at him. After several moments of applause Mr Braddock raised his hands. It was quiet.

"Now ladies and gentlemen! The boy is going to perform spectacular and amazing feats of skill and daring underwater."

Mr Arnold laughed. "Get your pennies ready, folks."

"Are you ready, boy?" Mr Braddock said. "All right then. On with the show!"

"On with the show!" the Arnold children yelled, jumping up and down. "On with the show! On with the show!" Mrs Arnold stood up and took their hands and then it was suddenly perfectly quiet in the yard.

Benjamin cleared his throat. He walked slowly toward the edge of the pool, keeping his chin down against his chest so he could see where he was going through the mask, but before he reached the water one of his flippers got caught under his foot and he nearly pitched forward onto his face. The children began to laugh again and leap up and down.

"Oh no," Mrs Arnold said. "That wasn't funny."

"Hey Ben," Mr Arnold called. "Be careful when you come up. You don't want to get the bends."

Benjamin placed his foot down onto the top step at the shallow end of the pool, then walked slowly down the steps to the pool's floor.

"Wait a minute," his father said. He hurried to the edge of the pool with the spear, Benjamin stared at him a moment through the glass, then grabbed the spear away from him, turned around and began walking slowly down the slope of the pool toward the deep end. The water rose up around his black suit to the level of his chest. Then to his neck. Just as the water level was at his chin the flippers began scraping against the bottom of the pool. He let all his breath out and tried to force himself under but the air tank kept him afloat. He began thrashing with his arms but his head would not go under. The Arnold children began to laugh. Finally he turned around and began moving slowly back up toward the shallow end. The neighbors in back began booing through the fence. By the time he reached the steps everyone in the yard was booing except for his father, who was standing at the head of the pool frowning at him.

Benjamin pulled the mask partially away from his face. "The show's over," he said quietly.

7 **feat** *here:* demonstration
7 **daring** courage
21 **the bends** *(informal)* a painful condition that divers get when they come up too quickly
22 **shallow** *opp. of* deep
31 **afloat** on top of the water
31 **to thrash** to hit wildly
37 **to frown at s.o.** to look angrily at s.o.
38 **partially** ['pɑ:ʃəlɪ]

"What's wrong?"

"He needs a weight!" Mr Arnold called. "That'll get him under. If you had a big rock it would do it."

"Right," Mr Braddock said. He straightened up. "Folks?" he said. "There will be a brief intermission. Hang on to your seats." He hurried past the pool and through a gate into the rear part of the yard, where the incinerator was.

Benjamin stood quietly at the shallow end of the pool resting the end of his spear on the pool's floor and staring through his mask at Peter Arnold. It was perfectly quiet. When Mr Braddock returned he was carrying a large piece of concrete used to keep the lid of the incinerator closed. Benjamin took it from him and walked slowly back toward the deep end. Some of the guests began laughing and applauding as his head went under and then it was perfectly quiet beneath the water as he walked gradually down to the very bottom of the pool. He stood a moment looking at a wall of the pool, then sat down. Finally he eased himself down onto his side and balanced the heavy piece of concrete on his hip. Then he turned his head to look up at the shiny, silver surface of the pool above. "Dad?" he said quietly into his mask.

45 **intermission** break in a performance

47 **incinerator** a container for burning rubbish

51 **concrete** ['--] ⚠ building material made from cement *(Beton)*

55 **to ease o.s.** to move very carefully

The Graduate by Charles Webb, Penguin, 1963, pp. 35–36.

Understanding a novel extract ▶

1. What impression does the text give of the father-son relationship?
2. How do the guests and neighbours behave?
3. a) Do you think this scene is funny? Why, or why not?
   b) Explain the meaning of the ending.
4. a) "The novelist makes use of an *unobtrusive third-person narrator.*" Find examples in the novel extract which support this statement.
   b) What other types of third-person narrator do you know? In what way do they differ from the unobtrusive narrator?
5. a) How do you think father and son feel during the "performance"? Try to assign these feelings to specific parts of the text.
   b) Retell the final paragraph with Ben as the first-person narrator who clearly voices his thoughts and feelings about the situation.

An unobtrusive third-person narrator

gives an objective description of the action without any information about the characters' thoughts and feelings. The reader hardly notices this narrator as he/she hides behind a seemingly neutral presentation of events.

Screenplay extract

Mr Braddock moves to the screen door and pushes it open. It slams against the wall inside.

MR BRADDOCK – Benjamin Braddock!

Int. Braddock Breakfast Kitchen – Shot Down the Hall / Day

At the back of the hall, inside the house, stands Ben, dressed in a full length skin diver's wet suit, flippers on his feet, the oxygen tank strapped to his back, the mask pushed up his forehead, the air hose dangling. He holds a spear gun in his hand. The people applaud.

Ext. Braddock Backyard and Pool Area – Day Shot – From Ben's POV

The people in the backyard. His father stands just outside the screen door.

MR BRADDOCK Folks – this remarkable young man is going to perform for you some spectacular and amazing feats of daring in water that is over six feet deep –

4 **int.** *short for* interior, *here:* inside a building

8 **to dangle** to hang loosely

9 **ext.** *short for* exterior, *here:* outside a building

9 **POV** (camera) point of view

10 **screen door** a door with metal netting which keeps insects out

Ben's arms come into view and pull the mask down.
We are now looking through the mask as we move forward down the hall. Everything is slightly distorted through the glass. Ben's hand comes up again with the breathing apparatus in it.
SOUND: the rhythmic pumping of air, obliterating the sound of the people around the pool who seem to be applauding and chattering noiselessly.
We move out of the door and toward the pool. Mr. Braddock is running back and forth, clapping his hands and delivering his now soundless pitch.
We move down the steps and into the shallow end of the pool. Mr. Braddock is moving along the side of the pool, motioning toward us to come down to the deep end. He joins Mr. Arnold at the far end of the pool. They both begin to motion us toward them.
We get to the deep end of the pool. Mr. Braddock signals us with his hand to go under. He kneels down by the edge of the pool and reaches out with his hand and pushes us under. He has a big smile.
We surface again and pan around for a last look. The figures, through the slightly distorted glass of the mask of Mrs. Arnold and Mrs. Braddock, watching and smiling; the neighbors on each side of the house, looking over their fences and laughing and pointing; Mr. Arnold nodding encouragement and talking; Mr. Braddock on his knees, smiling and trying to reach out far enough to push us under. We go under and sink to the bottom of the pool.
Ext. Braddock Backyard and Pool Area – Day Overhead Shot (Helicopter POV)
Looking down on the pool, on Ben's black-suited body at the bottom and the people standing around the pool, looking down into it.
Pull up and up and up.
Until there are thirty houses below us, with their owners, swimming, playing, eating, cooking, reading, dancing, sunbathing, constructing and gardening around thirty pools.

17 **distorted** making objects look unclear

19 **to obliterate the sound** to keep the sound out completely
24 **pitch** *here:* commentary

The Graduate, screenplay by Buck Henry, 1967, Lawrence Turman Inc.

◀ **Novel and film**

1. a) Which cinematic point of view corresponds to the unobtrusive third-person narrator? Why? Which camera shots project an objective point of view? Which shots project a subjective point of view? See page 112 for help with your answer.

Cinematic point of view

Cinematic point of view depends on the position of the camera. It may be:
– *objective*: The camera is like a "window" through which the viewer observes people and events.
– *subjective:* The camera shows the action from the viewpoint of a film character, e.g. through his/her eyes or over his/her shoulder.

b) How can a director suggest a character's feelings and thoughts? Think of body language, camera operations, music, lighting, slow motion, voice-overs, etc.

2. a) Find parallels between the novel extract and the shooting script of the birthday scene (action, dialogue, characters). Then, using a grid like the one below, show the differences between the two texts:

	novel extract	shooting script
action		
dialogue		
characters		

b) Sum up your notes. What has been added to, omitted from or simplified in the shooting script? Are there any shifts of emphasis? What could be the reasons for the changes?
c) In general, are you happy with the scriptwriter's version of the birthday scene? Why, or why not?

3. a) What information does the shooting script give us about camera operations?
b) Try to fill in any "gaps" in the shooting script, e.g. give a precise description of what you imagine the actors/actresses to look like.

4. Watch the film scene twice. How close is it to the shooting script?

A step further ▶

- a) Watch the beginning of *The Graduate* and the scene with the graduation party, which comes directly afterwards. Working in four groups, take notes on one of the following aspects: camera operations (cf. page 112), the protagonist, the dialogue, the setting.
b) Analyse a film scene of your choice. You can refer to pages 113–114 for more ideas about in-depth film analysis.
- a) Think of an example of a film which uses one of the following devices:
flashbacks – a voice-over – slow motion.
b) What effects can you produce by using these techniques in a film?
c) Write a voice-over text spoken by (an older) Ben Braddock to introduce the party scene.

Flashback
A film scene showing events in the past. It is included in the film present.

Voice-over
The voice of a narrator speaking offscreen.

project ▶

- Write a shooting script for one of the dramatic or prose texts in this book, e.g. "Make your lives extraordinary" *(Dead Poets Society)* or "The black-haired girl" *(What's Eating Gilbert Grape)*. You could film your version and if possible, compare it to the original film version.
- Suggest a sequence of shots with alternating objective and subjective points of view for a typical scene in a Western in which a stagecoach is being attacked by bandits. See page 112 "Camera operations" for help.
Useful words/phrases: stage driver – to hold and slap reins – to look back over his shoulder – to scream at the horses – heads in profile – bandits follow in hot pursuit – to chase/to catch up with the coach – fear – determination – exhaustion

WB: pp. 55–56

Youth in the media

Two newspaper articles

- a) What mood does the drawing create? How?
  b) Find a caption for the drawing.
  c) What do you think the article it illustrates is about?
- In groups, make a topic web on newspapers. See page 120 for help.

WB: p. 15, Dilemma

1. Read the headlines of both articles. Look up any words you don't know.
   a) What makes these headlines interesting?
   b) What do you expect the articles to be about?
2. Divide into groups. Each group should read one of the articles. Don't forget, the context will help you to understand the meaning of some of the unknown words.

Drawing by Riddell, *The Observer*, 25 June, 1995.

The children who live in fear of the yobs

Barry Hugill and Ruth Fisher

Children in British cities live in daily fear of violence. Youngsters are terrified of school bullies, playground drug-dealers and violent gangs.

A year-long study of Manchester children, the largest ever in Britain, confirms that thousands of children find the world a frightening and threatening place. It follows previous studies showing bullying to be endemic in schools. And it provides further evidence to police claims, first reported in *The Observer*, that few schools are free of drug dealers.

Manchester City Council has been consulting children aged 8-14. Young people from all social classes and ethnic groups were asked what most worried them. The findings have shocked officials. They discovered a generation terrified of growing up without a job or a home. Time and again children expressed fear about violence at school and on the streets. Racial attacks were often mentioned – not only whites attacking blacks, but inter-racial fighting and bullying.

The findings will be published next month. Officials insist it is a 'snapshot' rather than a scientific survey. Nevertheless, 2,500 children – 8 per cent of the age group – filled in questionnaires and thousands more took part in discussion groups.

Officials say this does not mean it is unsafe to walk the streets of Manchester; rather that children think it is. The finding is consistent with a nationwide study of parents conducted last year by the Policy Studies Institute, which found parents terrified of letting children out on their own because of fear of assault, abduction or injury from traffic. In 1971, 80 per cent of children took themselves to school – today the figure is 9 per cent.

Margaret Smith, a senior Manchester official said: 'We have a lost generation of youngsters. They are telling us they want safe places to play. They want parks, youth clubs and places you can go to where there is no alcohol and no drugs. Life is tough for them, and it is getting tougher.' The survey will be published at about the time of the Conservative Party conference and will fuel the debate about law and order and the 'yob culture'. Manchester is committed to a 'prevention is better than cure' approach and wants to increase spending on play schemes and youth projects. [...]

14 **endemic** [en'demɪk] *here:* found everywhere – 16 **evidence** ['---] – 17 **claim** *here:* statement, report – 30 **time and again** repeatedly, often – 51 **consistent with** ⚠ [-'--] in agreement with – 76 **to fuel** [fjʊəl] *here:* to intensify

By Barry Hugill and Ruth Fisher, *The Observer*, 25 September, 1994.

Tamed by tough talk

Hardline way to cure delinquency

School deals: An answer to trouble such as violence

TERROR tot John graduated in almost every classroom crime imaginable between his fifth and 14th birthdays.

His school reports recorded violence, vandalism and football hooliganism, yet showed he was unable to read or write properly.

He was the youngest of five children from a troubled north London home, attended a primary school for emotionally disturbed pupils, and was given special child guidance at secondary school before most teachers wrote him off as a hopeless case.

He appeared destined to become one more among thousands of juvenile delinquents who would rise through the ranks of criminality to fill the nation's police cells, courts and prisons.

But *The Impossible Child* (Trentham Books, £8.95), a 256-page book being published this month, argues that tough talking and hard bargaining, rather than wishy-washy counselling, offer the only real chance of keeping classroom troublemakers like him on the straight and narrow.

Author David Lane, director of the Professional Development Foundation, investigated more than 3,000 such cases of delinquency, of which 250 were closely tracked.

He said: 'Being soft doesn't work. Hard bargaining does. Pupils like John want to know: "What's the deal?"'

Watched

'They need to have it spelled out to them what is right and wrong, what is acceptable and unacceptable, and what will happen to them if they break their part of the bargain.

'But they must also be monitored intensely to make sure that if they make a deal, they stick to it to the letter.'

John proved a case in point, he said. As a last resort, teachers laid down the law by agreeing a 'contract' with the wayward pupil and his mother.

Mr Lane said: 'It was very clear, stating exactly what behaviour was expected and what the consequences would be if the conditions were not met.'

John was effectively put on probation for nine months.

His work and behaviour were constantly watched by staff to see if he stepped out of line. He did so only twice in that time.

The teachers also agreed to deal with any action against him by other pupils during his probation. Mr Lane said: 'Five years after leaving school he is now holding down a steady job as a garage mechanic.

'In other circumstances he could have been facing a string of convictions and a life of prison.'

Mr Lane says teachers must learn that you sometimes have to be cruel to be kind. 'Where there is concrete, pragmatic and practical help, there is change.' [...]

From *The Daily Mail* (Education Notebook), 3 July, 1990.

2 **delinquency** [-'---] wrong-doing – 3 **tot** [ɒ] *(informal)* young child – 3 **to graduate** *here:* to be good at – 11 **disturbed** [-'-] – 13 **to write s.o. off** to decide s.o. is useless – 19 **to rise … of criminality** to commit increasingly bad crimes – 28 **bargaining** ['bɑːɡɪnɪŋ] trying to reach an agreement (usu. when selling s.th.) – 29 **wishy-washy** ['wɪʃɪˌwɒʃɪ] – 33 **on the straight and narrow** under control, behaving correctly – 41 **to track** *here:* to follow carefully – 48 **to spell out** to explain clearly – 55 **to monitor** to control and lead – 57 **to the letter** exactly, without exceptions – 59 **case in point** typical example – 60 **as a last resort** when nothing else worked – 63 **wayward** uncontrollable – 70 **to meet the conditions** *here: to* fulfil the contract – 76 **staff** [stɑːf] *here:* teachers – 89 **string** *here:* series

1. In your groups, work on the article you have read.
   a) Find headings for each sense unit within the text. Make sure that your expressions are neutral.
   b) Transform the article into a short *news item* to inform the other groups of the contents of the article. Make your text as concise as possible. Think of a short and eye-catching headline.
2. Present your news items in class.
   a) Compare them with the expectations all of you had when reading the headlines.
   b) Discuss how you decided what information to include in the news item with the other groups that read the same article.
3. On the basis of the information in the box, explain what kind of article you have analysed.
4. a) Which of the two articles is taken from a serious newspaper, which from a popular paper?
   b) Make a chart, listing as many characteristics as possible for each type of paper.

- "Tamed by tough talk" may have caused different people to write letters to the editor, for example: parents with problem children supporting the methods described; a pupil complaining that troublemakers are given too much attention; a young person who dropped out because nobody seemed to care when he/she went to school…
  a) Together, think of other perspectives.
  b) In small groups, or with a partner, choose one of the perspectives and write a letter to the editor. See page 118 for further help.
  c) In class, discuss which of the letters the editor might print and why.
- Discuss what advice you could give to younger pupils on how to cope with bullying.

◀ Reading and comparing

Newspaper articles

News reports deal with events of general importance in an objective way, concentrating on the five "w's": who, what, when, where, why; sometimes also: how. They usually answer these questions in the first paragraph, then add details and background information in further self-contained paragraphs.

News items answer these questions usually in one concise paragraph.

News stories may also include the reporter's personal impressions and opinions and/or quotations from eye-witnesses and experts.

WB: pp. 6–7, Grammar review; p. 15, Committing an offence

What atmosphere does this photo from a newspaper create? What do you think has happened? What might the boy be thinking?

VERONICA BIRKETT

Let's be tough on crime: teach children to love themselves

My job involves supporting special-needs children in mainstream schools, and I'm sitting around a table with a group of seven-year-olds.

We have worked together for some months on their reading skills, and they are progressing well. I decide the time has come to ask a crucial question: "Tell me, what are you good at?"

Responses come in the form of startled looks, suspicion, confusion and, finally, one voice expressing the unspoken thoughts of the others: "I'm no good at anything." Low self-esteem? Absolutely.

So why do I think self-esteem is the key to the nation's problems? By "problems" I mean the explosion in the crime rate and growing number of young people involved in drug and alcohol abuse.

The Government's answer appears to lie in spending large amounts of public money on extending the prison service, on advertising campaigns about the dangers of drugs and drink, and on creating rehabilitation centres. But these measures do not work, as we can see from the statistics.

Now, join me with another group – this time of 17-year-olds from a secure unit. All have been involved in crime, and have drug- or alcohol-related problems. Pose the same question, "Tell me, what are you good at?" and you receive the same response – only the "I'm no good at anything" will be more vehement because they have experienced a further 10 years of failure.

Young people with low self-esteem are vulnerable. If they have no love or respect for themselves, they will have none for others. They will be tempted into crime as one way of gaining attention and stimulation; and, as they have little care for themselves or others, what have they got to lose?

So what, if the use of drugs or alcohol is damaging to the body and may lead to anti-social behaviour? At least it blots out the pain of failure. What value does life have anyway?

I do not want my little group of struggling seven-year-olds to lead lives of pain, despair and frustration, but already they are showing signs of feeling worthless. We must devise ways of preventing young people from developing these feelings of inadequacy in the first place.

Most of the leading psychological bodies accept that we are all influenced by early childhood experiences. We reached decisions about our own worth first through messages received from adults, then from our peer groups. Surely we should see what we can do to ensure that children today receive positive, empowering messages.

Instead of the Government having to spend vast amounts on "picking up the pieces", could it not spend much less on national schemes aimed at promoting self-esteem?

An obvious start would be the introduction of parenting-skills classes, at present available to all pregnant women. Then teachers could be trained to develop children's self-esteem, and whole-school policies, aimed at helping children to feel good about themselves, could become part of the national curriculum – essential, not optional.

If parenting skills were taught to pupils in their final years, they might leave school with some awareness of the implications for the child and its family of an irresponsible and ineffective upbringing.

If these ideas were taken seriously and put into practice, we might all be able to look forward to living in a safer and less hostile world.

By Veronica Birkett, *The Independent,* 21 November, 1994.

3 **mainstream** normal, conventional – 12 **crucial** ['kru:ʃl] extremely important – 22 **esteem** [-'-] respect – 40 **measure** *here:* action taken to improve s.th. – 45 **secure unit** prison for young criminals – 55 **vehement** ['vi:əmənt] strong, forceful – 59 **vulnerable** ['vʌlnrəbl] easy to hurt – 74 **to blot out** to remove – 84 **to devise** [dɪ'vaɪz] to plan – 108 **scheme** ⚠ [ski:m] plan, project – 109 **to promote** *here:* to support – 123 **essential** [ɪ'senʃl] *here:* required – 137 **hostile** ['hɒstaɪl] unfriendly, aggressive

Reading and thinking

1. a) What kind of article did you expect when reading the headline? Were your expectations fulfilled?
   b) What is unusual about the first three paragraphs?
2. Which characteristic elements of a *feature* can you find in the whole article?
3. What is Veronica Birkett aiming to do in her article? You might want to refer to the box below.

The author's aims

The author's aims can influence the style of writing. In some texts one of the following aims will dominate, others contain several such elements:
– *Description:* the author describes what a place, object or person looks like in detail so that the reader can imagine it clearly.
– *Exposition:* the reader is given information or explanations.
– *Narration:* the author relates an event or a sequence of events. (Novels, short stories, etc. are narrative texts; reports and newspaper articles contain narrative elements.)
– *Argumentation:* the author tries to convince the reader by means of carefully reasoned arguments (pros and cons).
– *Persuasion:* the author tries to influence the reader's opinions or actions by supporting one point of view, often in an emotional rather than a rational way. (Speeches usually mix argumentative and persuasive elements; adverts are persuasive).
– *Instruction:* the reader is taught what to do or how to do something.

Feature

Features are articles on topics of general interest rather than 'hot' news. Writers of features not only investigate problems but they also give background to news stories.

A step further

- a) If Veronica Birkett were running for the office of a city councillor, what do you think she would write on a handout to be distributed in town?
  b) What sort of advert would she publish in the local papers? See page 115.
- Write a letter to the editor (see page 118 of this book and WB: page 42) expressing one of the following views on juvenile troublemakers:
  "The politicians are to be blamed because they do not spend enough money on youth."
  "Television and videos are to be blamed because they make light of violence and present aggression as an adequate means to settle conflicts."
  a) Collect evidence and arguments in groups.
  b) Write your letter to the editor individually. Make sure it is obvious which article you are writing about.
  c) Discuss which of your letters might have a chance of being printed.
- Conduct a panel discussion on the reasons for the increase in the number of juvenile troublemakers. See page 106 for further help.

WB: p. 19, Youth – trouble or troubled?

project

Your class has been asked to publish a special edition of your school newspaper to inform your partner school in Great Britain or the U.S.A. about your school in order to convince more pupils to take part in the exchange programme. See "Producing a newspaper" on page 122 of this book and WB: page 33.

The camera doesn't lie...?

Getting started ▶

> **Advertising**
> **Advertisements** (**adverts, ads**) are notices or film sequences designed to sell products, e.g. in newspapers and magazines, on television. **Commercials** are advertisements on television or radio.

- a) Look at the photos on pages 52 and 53. Do you think that they show models who are posing, or do they show real-life situations? Give reasons.
  b) What is the function of the photos?
- Look through newspapers and magazines for articles about young people. What themes are discussed in these articles? If the article is accompanied by a photo, what images does it create of young people?

▶ *The following freeze frames are taken from a commercial for* The Guardian, *a British quality newspaper. The commercial shows an event from three angles. The scenes are frozen briefly to allow viewers to form an opinion.*

1. a) Work in pairs. Each pair concentrates on just one of the two photos on the left.
   – Describe the situation and the young man in the photo.
   – Think of a short caption for the photo as it might appear in a newspaper.
   b) Work with a pair which looked at the same photo as you. Compare your descriptions and captions.
2. Discuss the image of youth these photos create. To what extent do you think this image is based on prejudice?

3. a) What makes the third frame in the sequence surprising?
   b) Comment on the camera angle and field size in the third photo compared to the first two frames. See page 112 for help.
4. In your opinion, what image of the *Guardian's* reporting style is the commercial trying to convey?
5. a) In the commercial, a voice-over comments briefly on each frame. In groups, write the script for the voice-over as you imagine it to have been. Don't forget to mention *the Guardian* in your script.
   b) Compare your results with the other groups. Which script:
   – gives the most positive picture of the *Guardian*?
   – is most likely to be remembered?

A step further ▶

- If your school has the *Mad for Ads 2* video, look at the *Guardian* ad.
  a) What makes it effective? Examine in particular the relationship between the film sequence and the voice-over (the speaker in the background).
  b) What advantages does a video version have over a possible print version?
- Turn the events in the photos above into a news item for the local television network. You could include short, on-the-spot interviews with the three people, in which they give their feelings both at the time and now. Read out your news report and act out the dialogues.

> **WB:** p. 50, How to present a commercial in class

Tough – just the way you like it

Getting started

- a) What kind of products are advertised on television by young adults?
  b) Think of slogans, in English, which are used to appeal to this age group. What is the message of the slogan in each case?

Looking and thinking

1. Describe the situation in the above advert. Is it unrealistic, romantic, amusing…? Give reasons for your answer.
2. What is going to happen in the next few seconds? What do you think the two people will be doing in an hour's time?
3. What brand image is the product given? (See the box on the right.)
4. a) Comment on the composition of the photo and the position of the logo and tag line in the advertisement. (See also page 94 "Talking about advertisements II" for ideas.)
   b) Do you think that the brand name and logo will stick in people's minds? Say why or why not.

- Turn the Baby-G ad into a 30-second television commercial.
  – Develop a simple plot and sketch the important shots as freeze frames.
  – Make a storyboard. (Look at page 114 for help.)
  – Write a short script for a voice-over. Find a suitable piece of music or a song to play in the background.
  – Rehearse the commercial and tape it.
- If the *Mad for Ads 2* video is available in your school, look at advert no. 3.
  a) What parallels are there between the Sony Handycam and the Baby-G ads?
  b) What is the message of the Handycam commercial? How is it conveyed? Comment on the voice-over, the changes in perspective, the storyline, etc.

Talking about advertisements I

(advertising) copy: *text of an ad excluding the headline and tag line*
tag line: *short, catchy summary of the message in an ad*
logo: *product symbol*
slogan: *concise phrase associated with a product*
brand image: *positive image evoked by the product*

Heartbreak High

Soap operas (soaps) are radio or television serials with continuing stories and many parallel plots. They are about events and problems in the lives of ordinary characters. Episodes usually have an open ending to make viewers curious about the next one.

- If you were to plan a *soap opera* about a school:
  - what type of school would you choose?
  - what kind of students and teachers would need to be involved to make for an interesting plot? Think of an interesting cast.
  - what events and problems could it deal with?
  - what role would teachers and parents play?

▶ Heartbreak High *is the name of a popular Australian weekly soap. It deals with events at Hartley High School. These freeze frames and transcripts are taken from the pilot film. You are going to meet two new students.*

Declan: "Don't catch a chill Mum!"

Kat: "You must admit he's kind of irresistible."

***Declan** got into trouble at his last school and was expelled. The teachers at Hartley High are going to give him a second chance. Declan's father is dead and he lives with his mother who is ill.*

Looking and thinking ▶

1. What do the freeze frames and the captions tell us about Declan?
2. What kind of storylines might a scriptwriter develop for this character?

***Stassy** is just starting at Hartley High. It is her first day.*

Looking and thinking ▶

3. Describe the first impression you have of Stassy.
4. a) Speculate on her reasons for changing her looks in the photo on the right.
   b) How do you think you would react if Stassy came to your class as a new pupil?
5. a) Describe the camera angles used in the photos. (See page 112 for help.)
   b) How effective are these angles in describing Stassy's situation?
6. What kind of music would you choose to go with the scenes?

Now read what some other characters say about Stassy later in the day.

ALLIE (pupil): Maybe she just prefers her own company.
KAT: Maybe she's just full of herself.

******

MR BELL (teacher): Apparently she's from a very strict Yugoslav family. Something about her eyes. I got the shock of my life when she came into class. All that grunge. Why do they do it?
MRS BROOKS (teacher): Fashion…
MR BELL: Fashion!
MRS BROOKS: Sometimes it's a good place to hide.
MR BELL: Hide? What has she got to hide from?
MRS BROOKS: She's a gorgeous girl. That can make it really hard for her.
MR BELL: Yeah, well…

2 **she is full of herself** she only thinks of herself

5 **grunge** untidy fashion associated with fans of **grunge** (rock music with punk and heavy metal elements)

10 **gorgeous** ['gɔ:dʒəs] very good-looking

◀ **Looking and thinking**

7. How do these remarks change, or add to, the impression you already had of Stassy?
8. How do you think the storyline with Stassy might continue? Suggest a few scenes with Stassy and some of the pupils and/or the teachers which would drive the plot.

Kat, Declan and Stassy

The following conversation takes place later on in the episode. Kat has been asked by Mr Bell to find a locker for Stassy. She is not happy about this as she has other things on her mind.

KAT: Oh Declan!
DECLAN: *(clearly unwilling to talk to her)* Yeah?
KAT: Hi. You did a really good job with the bunsen burners today.
DECLAN: What do you want?
KAT: Nothing. Science has always been my weakest subject, and you seem to be really good at it.
DECLAN: Having a genuine interest does help.
STASSY: *(trying to find locker, to Kat)* Um … I'm sorry, but can you tell me which one's supposed to be mine?
KAT: Any one that's empty.
STASSY: Well, could you tell who I'm supposed to see about getting a key?
KAT: How do I know?
DECLAN: I'll get you a key. In the meantime you can chuck your stuff in my locker if you want.
STASSY: Oh no, it's alright. I'll hang on to it if you don't mind.
DECLAN: Sure. See you in the yard. *(leaves)*
STASSY: Thanks.
KAT: Nice moves, Catwoman. I couldn't have done it better myself. I'm in awe really.
STASSY: Pardon?

"Nice moves, Catwoman."

19 **nice moves** *(here: negative)* actions planned to achieve s.th.
19 **Catwoman** character in a *Batman* film
20 **in awe** [ɔ:] *(here: sarcastic)* full of respect and wonder

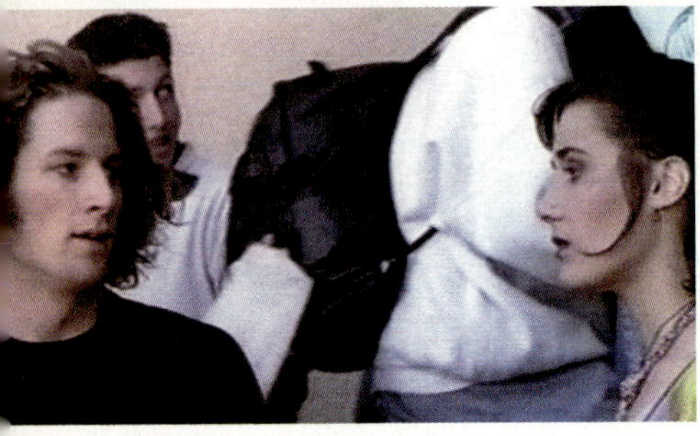
"Don't let Kat bother you!"

KAT: Lunch is that way. Follow your nose and have a nice life. Oh … and welcome to Hartley High.

Cut to school yard

DECLAN: Do you want to come and shoot some baskets with us?

STASSY: No, … thanks anyway.

DECLAN: Don't let Kat bother you.

Looking and thinking ▶

9. Visualize the relationships between Stassy, Declan and Kat using a triangle in which the thickness of the lines shows the quality of the relationships. See the example on page 15.
10. In groups outline how you expect these relationships and the plot to develop. Present your results in class and decide which plot is:
    - the most plausible.
    - most likely to get viewers to watch the next episode.

A step further ▶

- If the video is available in your school, watch the whole episode of *Heartbreak High* in class. Then, consider the following points.
  - Compare it with the expectations you had after analysing the freeze frames. Which conflicts had you anticipated, which came as a surprise?
  - How many plots can you detect in the episode? Find titles for them. Then, working in groups, examine one of the plots in detail. How might it be continued in the next episode?
  - Look at the box on soap operas on page 58. Which typical characteristics of a soap opera did you notice in the episode of *Heartbreak High*?
- Prepare and give a one-minute talk on the following topic: "Soaps are like real life – only more so". You could look at page 107 for help.
- Think of German soap operas about young people that you know. You could tape an episode of one soap for comparison purposes. In what ways is *Heartbreak High* different? Consider the characters, storylines, setting, possible cultural differences and the budget available.

project ▶

Find out how youth is presented in music videos.

1. Tape videos of English songs that deal with love or friendship.
2. Work in small groups. Try to choose a video that shows an interesting or typical image of teenage love. Prepare a presentation of your video in class.
   - Decide what makes the video interesting, e.g. the image of the singer/group, the lyrics, the storyline, the mood created by the pictures and the music.
   - Prepare questions about the clip or tasks that the rest of the class can do while watching it. Ask your teacher for advice if necessary.
3. Present your video in class and then discuss the following points:
   - What ideas about teenage relationships do they have in common, where do they differ?
   - What clichés regarding gender role, if any, are reflected in the video?

WB: p. 49, How to present a video clip in class

Media workshop

If you want to look at a specific area of media in more detail, choose one of the following projects and take over a lesson! You will find help on pages 114–115. First, you will need to find someone in your class who can tape suitable material in English. You could also ask a penfriend or your partner school or pupils you know who are on an exchange trip abroad for help in getting material. There is often interesting material on the Internet, too.

Youth in the news and documentaries

◄ project

1. When you have found interesting material about young people, prepare it for presentation in class. You can use the grid below to help you organize your notes. See page 112–114 for help with film analysis.

topic/aspects	What is the main topic? What aspects are discussed?
film material used	Do the pictures speak for themselves? Is the material staged or authentic? Give examples. What other information is given? E.g. charts, maps
spoken material	Can you hear dialogues between people? Are there any interviews? Are experts asked for an opinion?
voice-over/ pictures	What is the function of the voice-over? Does it describe the pictures or give extra information, too? How necessary are the pictures for an understanding of the topic?
balanced or biased?	Is a controversial topic presented from different angles? Is a full range of opinions presented? Are viewers given a variety of information to enable them to draw their own conclusions or does a speaker evaluate the information? Is the speaker's voice neutral or is it emotional in some way?

2. Decide on the best method of presenting the material.
   - If the material is easy to understand, the class could watch it and discuss the gist. Then, watch it again, this time looking for more detail.
   - If the material is difficult, prepare your audience, e.g. ask general questions about the topic; hand out a text with gaps and a list of the missing words to be filled in; prepare a grid with key ideas which has to be filled in while, or after, watching the material.
   - Get a discussion going by turning off the sound. The class can speculate about the message. This is a good method if you feel the commentary is biased or there is a discrepancy between pictures and text.
   - Cover the screen so that the picture is not visible if the text is easy to understand and/or the pictures are redundant. Discuss the message of the commentary before showing the material again with the picture.

Newscasts
give brief information about topical events. They are usually read by a newsreader, and may be accompanied by visual material.

News reports
are more detailed than newscasts. They usually include film material and interviews e.g. by an on-the-spot reporter. He/she also provides up-to-the-minute information.

A documentary
is a film which explores, in detail, a subject of general interest, which may or may not be topical. It deals with real events and people, but its structure is similar to a film telling a story. It should be factual, accurate and well investigated. It also provides background information, e.g. interviews, archive material, statistics.

WB: p. 51, How to present a news item

3. a) Working in pairs or groups, discuss how young people are presented in these programmes. What role do they play in society?
   b) Discuss whether you agree/disagree with this picture of young people.
   c) How would you present your generation in a television documentary?

project ▶

Target group: Youth in soap operas, talk shows, music programmes, interactive programmes

You could deal with these kinds of programmes in the following ways:

- Think of examples of each kind of programme. What topics do they deal with? Do you find these programmes interesting, or not? Give reasons.
- Working in groups, develop a questionnaire to survey the viewing habits of pupils at your partner school(s) (see page 122 for help). You could put your questionnaire on the school homepage or take part in an Internet project with other schools.
- Analyse one or more episodes of a soap opera or talk show from an English-speaking country. Consider:
  - which topics, and especially 'typical' teenage problems, are dealt with.
  - what role models teenagers are presented with.
  - in what ways the material differs from similar German programmes.
- This is what a teenager said about the influence of television on her life: "They're feeding you a picture, and you want to be the same."
  Write down any ideas that come to mind in connection with this statement. Then, pool your ideas with the rest of the class.
- Discuss the importance of teenage soap operas, talk shows and interactive programmes for advertisers. Consider the following:
  - How much time is spent openly referring to products for teenagers?
  - How much *product placement* do you notice (see the box on the right)?
  - How many commercial breaks are there? How long are they compared to the actual programme?
  - To what extent are such programmes used to advertise and promote films, CDs or concerts?
  - How do music videos implicitly advertise a certain image of youth and the products connected with it?

Product placement
the inclusion of products and company logos in a film or television programme as a form of advertising

project ▶

Teen culture: music videos

- Look at how one of the following is dealt with in a music video of your choice: gender roles; the ideal world; dreams/nightmares.
  See page 115 for ideas. You could also get help from a class which does music at your school.

Music videos
may include a song and dance number or a concept performance (the band/singer are involved in illustrating the music and lyrics). A video may also be a concept clip video in which the soundtrack is combined with film material and the band/singer does not have a role in the video.

WB: p. 49, How to present a video clip in class

Learning for life

Playing God

- a) What does leaving home mean to you? Collect your ideas in a *mind map*. This is what the first stage of a mind map might look like. Continue it.

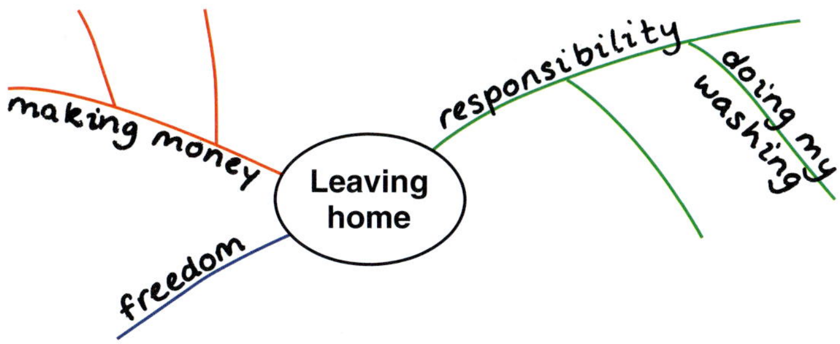

b) On the basis of your mind map, write a short text on what leaving home may mean. Plan each paragraph systematically.

- Choose one of the following topics to share a personal experience with the class:
  - An event that changed my life.
  - An event that changed the life of someone close to me.
  - What I would like to happen in order to change my life.

  Either describe it to the class on the basis of notes you have made, or write a poem and present it to the class. Remember not all poems have to follow a strict pattern. See "How to write a poem" on page 118.

▶ *When you read the following short story, try to work out the meaning of the words marked with numbers using the techniques described on p. 108 and WB, pp. 18–19. To help you, they have been summarized again on the right.*

He was almost to the river, walking fast, when he saw Laurel on her bicycle, racing to catch him. In a space between the gusts[3] of raw March wind she yelled, "Josh, wait up, or I'll break your legs."

So he wasn't going to get away without saying good-bye after all.

Laurel came puffing up[3], fierce and wind-whipped[3]. He braced himself as she stared at the duffel bag he'd taken from his folks' closet and stuffed[3] with all the clothes and things he thought he'd need.

"You're doing it," she said. The pain that came into her eyes hurt him, too. "Why? Without telling me? I thought we were friends! If I hadn't seen you sneaking through the alley –"

We are friends, he wanted to assure[3] her. Best friends. The best. But he said, walking on, "So? One more thing I didn't do right today." Suddenly it came pouring out. "At breakfast they jumped down my throat[3] about my grades. Then they got started on why can't I grow up and shape up[3] and do my part now with him out of work. Boy. I didn't get him laid off."

"But it's a hard time for them, Josh."

"Not for her. She's tickled pink. All this schooling's going to get her back into that career she gave up when I came along." It seemed vital to

Before you read

Mind map

A *mind map* shows what comes to mind automatically when you think of a certain expression. To note down your associations, it helps to move from the general to the more specific.

WB: p. 38, How to write poems

Surviving without a dictionary

1 refers to *word family*
2 refers to *similar German, French or Latin words*
3 refers to *context*

5 **to brace o.s.** to gather strength, because you expect s.th. unpleasant
6 **closet** ⚠ ['--] *(AE)* cupboard
10 **to sneak** to walk carefully and quietly so as not to be noticed
10 **alley** ⚠ narrow street
15 **to get laid off** to lose one's job
17 **to be tickled pink** *(informal)* to be very pleased
18 **vital** ⚠ ['vaɪtl] very important

Surviving without a dictionary

1 refers to *word family*
2 refers to *similar German, French or Latin words*
3 refers to *context*

stay cold and angry. Even with Laurel. Especially with Laurel, because she knew what he really was. "So I figured[3] I've been enough trouble – I might as well get on out there and do something with my life." He stared at the distant river waiting to be crossed.

"It's dumb," Laurel said, with the directness they had never been afraid to use with each other. "They'll just haul[3] you back. Parents aren't perfect. You're feeling sorry for yourself." She stopped in the road, trying to make him turn around, rethink[1]. But he kept walking. "Please, Josh," she said behind him. "Don't do it."

"You're leaving," he said.

"But not until school's out. And I wouldn't be, if we didn't have to move out to the Coast."

"But you are," he said. It wasn't her fault, he knew. She couldn't make her own choices. But he could. "Maybe I'll see you in sunny Cal."

"How'll you live, without money?" she asked into the wind. "Josh? How'll you eat? It scares me."

He turned around. She was outlined against the far-off[1] knob of land called Throne of Kings, where they had sat one day in dusty autumn grass, growing quieter and quieter until their faces turned and their mouths touched in a kiss as intent and sunstruck[1] as the silent hawks gliding[3] over them.

His feet kept moving him backward. "Hey, just don't worry about me," he called. "Nobody else does. Okay?" She didn't answer but her eyelids blinked fast. He relented. "Would you come as far as the bridge with me?"

She shook her head. "I have to get back to the library. I'm supposed to be helping with the party right now."

Hearing her say she should be getting punch[2] and cookies ready for some stumpy old lady who wrote bad poetry, at the moment he was running away, gave him the new rush of anger he needed to turn around and march out of her life.

The river sprawled[3] ahead of him, more sand than water. There was an eeriness in what he was doing: leaving someone he cared so much about without ending it right. He wished she'd run after him. But what could she say?

When he got to the bridge he looked back, expecting to see her pedaling[2] away, but she stood in the road, her hair blowing across her funny freckled face.

The long bridge turned his footsteps hollow as he started across. He had planned to wait for the bus at the crossroad a mile or so farther on. Between wind gusts he found himself straining[3] to hear the hum[3] of traffic. But the only sound was closer, a small lonesome[1] squeak like a bird he didn't recognize, or something grating under the bridge.

When would they notice he'd left home? he wondered. Maybe they wouldn't even miss him.

Near the end of the bridge the sound got louder. He scanned[3] the sky and the flat brown horizon[2]. Then he leaned over the bridge rail and looked down into a cardboard box on the sand at the water's edge. A jumble of yips[3] and squeals came from something dark squirming inside it.

23 **dumb** [dʌm]

32 **Cal** California

38 **intent** [-ˈ-] paying great attention to s.th.

38 **hawk** large bird that catches small animals for food *(Habicht)*

42 **to relent** [-ˈ-] to give in

51 **eeriness** strange frightening atmosphere

56 **freckled** with a lot of small, light-brown spots

57 **to turn hollow** *here:* to make s.th. sound as if it comes from a hole

61 **to grate** to make a harsh, unpleasant sound, to scratch

67 **to squirm** to move quickly from side to side

He felt his muscles clamp[3] into knots. He had to catch a bus. He was this far. He had to straighten[1] up and walk on past whatever was down there crying for help. But he couldn't.

He glanced at Laurel. She hadn't moved. He went to the far end of the bridge and climbed down through the weeds. The box twitched as he bent warily and looked in.

Puppies. Five of them, no bigger than fuzzy mittens, crawling in their prison.

Josh drew a weary sigh and squatted[3] to touch them. They went silent, rooting[3] hungrily against his hands. He lifted up a soft black puppy with eyes that melted a hole in his heart, and dropped it back into the pile. "No," he warned them. "I can't do anything, you guys. No."

Their little claws[2] grated on the high sides of the box as they struggled to reach him. He saw Laurel hanging over the bridge rail. "What's down there, Josh?" she called.

"Five puppies," he called back.

She came scrambling[3] down. Her eyes were blazing. "What kind of gutless wonder would throw them into the river! Oh, look at them." She gathered[3] two against her cheeks.

"Maybe somebody couldn't take care of them," he said, trying to be fair. But it wasn't fair. He flicked[3] his hands angrily, staying aloof. "Didn't want to be bothered. So, plop, off the bridge."

"But it's cruel," she said. "It's sad. Like back in early times, in the book Miss Rainey gave you, remember? When people left the defective[2] babies on a mountain so if the gods wanted them saved they could do a miracle[2]." Suddenly she handed him a puppy. "And guess what – along came good old Josh."

"No," he said. "Dang – I've got a bus to catch!" He dropped the puppy into the heap, as trapped as it was. "Why me? What'll I do with the dumb things?"

"You said you've always wanted a dog. You just got five of your wishes." She looked at his eyes and stopped trying to make him smile. "Take them back into town and find them homes. There'll be another bus. If you still ..."

He followed her gaze down the road he should be striding[3] along, and turned helplessly to the box. "Want a nice puppy?" [...]

[He managed to find owners for four of the puppies and returned home with the last one.]

His dad was watching the news. He asked, "Where've you been?" without turning from the TV.

Josh felt the eeriness start again, matching the jumpy[1] light of the screen that lit the room. He took the puppy out of his jacket. It seemed like fate, really, because the one that had been left was the one whose tender eyes had grabbed his heart beside the river.

"What's that?" his dad said, when he noticed. "You can't keep a dog. Your mother's got too much to do already."

"She won't have to take care of it," Josh said, keeping his voice even

73 **warily** ['weərɪlɪ] cautiously, as if expecting danger
74 **mitten** kind of glove covering four fingers together and the thumb separately
76 **weary** ['wɪərɪ] tired
85 **gutless** without courage; having a weak character
88 **aloof** [-'-] distant, detached
95 **dang** *(slang)* damn
102 **gaze** steady look
106 **to match s.th.** to fit s.th. well
108 **fate** power believed to control everything that happens to human beings
112 **even** *here:* unemotional, controlled

113 **housebreaking** housetraining
113 **shot** injection of medicine
113 **tag** *here:* piece of metal on a dog's collar with its owner's name on it
114 **spaying** sterilizing (of animals)

125 **uneasily** uncomfortably, in an uncertain way

129 **commercial** *(AE)* television advertisement

131 **to warp** to change and look strange, twisted

140 **inaudible** [ɪn'ɔ:dəbl] not to be heard

By Ouida Sebestyen from *Visions,* New York: Dell Publishing, 1987, pp. 87–98.

and slow. "I will. Feeding and housebreaking and shots and tags and spaying and everything."

His dad looked at him a long time. "Talk is cheap," he said.

"I guess you're going to have to risk[2] it," Josh said, braced against the gaze.

His dad turned back to the news. "She can't do everything. The house, her schooling. She's got big dreams for herself. Give her a chance."

The puppy tried to crawl inside Josh's collar. He had to feed it. He had to buy a bag of something. "I live here too," he said. He felt for his ticket money. Maybe if he called Laurel she'd walk to the store with him and carry the pup while he lugged[3] home a bag of dog chow[3]. And they could talk. "Give me a chance too. Okay?"

His dad switched channels[2], uneasily, testing, rejecting. He doesn't know how to answer me, Josh thought. He doesn't know what to say to any of this – to not having a job, or to getting ahead of him, or to being my father.

A commercial came on. His dad said, watching it, "When I went into the army my folks kept my dog for me. They said he got lost. Ran away. But I was never sure." His face slowly warped in the shifting[3] light. "Maybe he tried to find me. Or maybe he got killed and they hated to tell me. So I never could be sure, you know? For a long time I used to listen to the dogs barking[3], off in town. For years, I guess. Hoping I'd hear him."

Josh stopped halfway to the door. Hesitantly[1] he came back, and sat on the arm of the couch, stroking the hungry puppy with his thumb[2]. He stared at the television like his dad, not seeing it. Even with the sound turned high, he caught himself trying to hear other things. The far-off whine of buses. The almost inaudible cries and urgings and answers coming from everywhere.

Reading and thinking ▶

1. Describe the conflict Josh is in.
2. Compare the relationship between Josh and Laurel and between Josh and his parents. You may also visualize the constellation of characters the way you did when discussing "Keep on running" (see page 15). Remember that relationships may change!

Talking about relationships I

a relationship with one's parents/family may be …
warm/close/friendly • impersonal/superficial • strained/hostile

to be close friends with s.o. • to enjoy s.o.'s company
to dislike s.o. • to (not) be on the same wavelength as s.o.
to get on s.o.'s nerves • to (not) get on well with s.o.
to (not) be on speaking terms with s.o.

a friendship may be based on (mutual) trust/respect

3. What does the setting contribute to the atmosphere of the story?
4. What do the puppies symbolize?
5. Write a brief plot summary of the story. See page 116 for help.
6. a) Most of what happens in the story is seen through Josh's eyes. Find those passages in which this is most obvious.
   b) What makes it clear to the readers that they are looking into Josh's mind? What effect does this have on them?
   c) Rewrite one of the passages. Use one of the following:
   – a *'selective' third-person narrator* who tells the story from Laurel's perspective;
   – one of the characters as first-person narrator. The box on page 27 will help you.

Talking about atmosphere

The atmosphere created by a setting may be…
peaceful • pleasant
friendly • romantic
optimistic • joyful
or
tense • gloomy
violent • melancholic
depressing • aggressive

'Selective' third-person narrator

In contrast to a first-person narrator ("I"), a third-person narrator is not a character in the narrative but stands outside it. He/She refers to the characters in the story as "he/she/they". A 'selective' third-person narrator presents the story through the eyes of one character (limited point of view).

Close-up: characterization

WB: p. 39, Defining characters

1. When you tell your family about a friend they have not met, what points do you mention? How do you 'characterize' them and make your family see what kind of person he/she is?
2. a) Divide up into small groups. Each group should choose a different character from "Mildred" or "Playing God":
   mother – father – Mildred – Susie
   Josh – Laurel – Josh's father
   b) What do you learn about your character when you read the story? Does he/she change during the story? Make notes on what your character is like and on the different means of characterization in the text. Support your views with reference to the text. See "How to quote"on page 116.
   c) Present your findings to the rest of the class and compare the means of characterization used. See "How to present group work" on page 106.
3. What other means could the author of a story use to present the characters?

- Write down Laurel's diary entry on this day.
- In pairs, write a conversation between Josh's parents about Josh, resulting in their decision to sit down with him to talk things over. Act it out in class. See WB: pages 45–46 "How to hold a conversation" 1 and 2 for ideas.
- Write a short story about Josh's father and his dog. See page 117 of this book for further help. You could also look at WB: pages 34–35, "How to write a 'plot' story/'slice-of-life' story" for ideas.

WB: pp. 6–7, Grammar review; p. 9, Reflections on "Playing God"

What sort of atmosphere does the photo create?
Does this photo capture the situation Josh is in? Why, why not?

Independence from the family?

Talking about statistics

bar chart 

pie chart 

graph
diagram

a total of
half of, one third of...
5 percent of...
5 times as many ... as

a significant number/increase/decrease
a negligible quantity
compared with/to...

to indicate
to prove

Reasons for leaving home by age first left

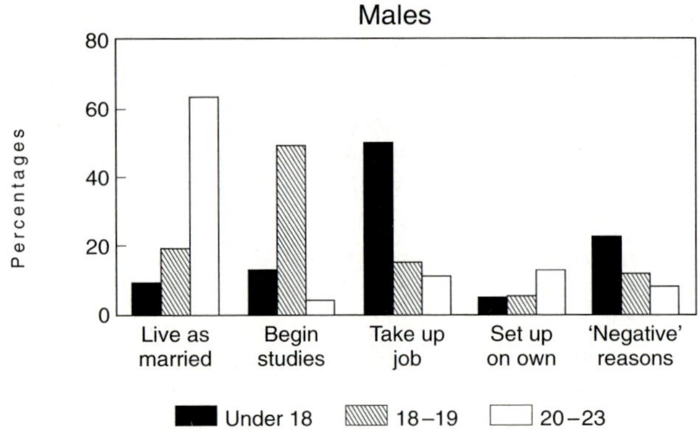

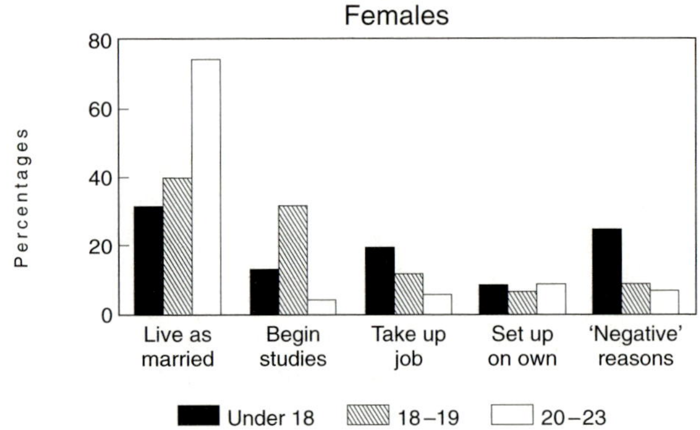

From *Youth, family and citizenship* by Gill Jones & Claire Wallace, Bristol: Open University Press, 1992, p. 109.

Looking and thinking ▶

1. Look at the statistics. Are the statements below correct?
   - Young women leave home to live with a partner earlier than young men.
   - Most people leave home when they come of age.
   - The reasons for people leaving home in their twenties are mainly private rather than career-oriented.
   - More young men than women are career-oriented.
   - The statistics are faulty because the total sum concerning an individual piece of information is higher than 100 per cent.
2. Compare and discuss your answers in class.
   a) Explain where in the statistics you found the information which is relevant for the statement.
   b) If your answer was wrong, find out what errors you made when interpreting the statistics, and why.
3. Draw your own conclusions from the statistics.

A step further: discussing ▶

- Discuss what statistics are good for.
- The writer Mark Twain wrote in his autobiography, "There are three kinds of lies: lies, damned lies, and statistics." Discuss this statement in class.

Off to London

Before you listen

- You want to move away from home, find a job in a big city and live with friends, but your parents disagree.
  a) Form three groups to find out the mother's/father's/son's or daughter's arguments.
  b) One person from each group now represents his/her case in a family conference. You could look at WB: p. 45 for useful vocabulary.
  c) Decide who has argued his/her case best, and why.

▶ *In the conversation you are going to hear, Sarah has just finished university and is now staying at her parents' house because her older sister, Louise, has recently got married. Sarah has just told her mother that she will be leaving home again to move to London, where she will share a flat with a friend.*
Before you listen to the recording, read the following annotations:
at one fell swoop *(fig.)* all of a sudden
drudge *(informal)* s.o. who works very hard at an unpleasant job

Listening for gist and atmosphere

1. The following nouns describe what a relationship between two people may be based on. Make sure you know what they mean.
   aggression – agreement – anxiety – care – concern – conflict
   guilt – habit – indifference – manipulation – mutual trust
2. Listen to the conversation without taking notes. Then discuss which of the nouns capture its atmosphere best.

Listening for detail: taking and using notes

1. Listen to the conversation again, this time taking notes on the details that support (or possibly change) your first impressions. See page 111 for help.
2. On the basis of your notes, discuss the following questions:
   a) Why does Sarah want to move out? How does she present her reasons?
   b) What reasons does her mother have to make her stay?
   c) What changes can you detect in their attitudes, and what do they reveal about their relationship?

A step further

- Discuss whose side you would take, and why.
- Choose one of the following tasks:
  a) Sarah writes to her London friend after deciding not to leave her mother;
  b) Sarah writes to her mother after leaving for London.
  See "How to write a letter" on page 118.
- One year later...
  a) In groups, imagine what Sarah's and her mother's situation will be like.
  b) Decide on one scenario. With a partner, write a suitable dialogue which can be made into part of a radio play. See page 117 for help and WB: page 45 for useful vocabulary.

WB: p. 40, How to write a personal letter

WB: p. 12, Text quiz; p. 27, Expressing certainties

"Mr and Mrs Ackerman, I'll come to the point. I'm deeply in love with your daughter, and I'd like to move in with you."

"It's my home too!"

- Describe the situation captured by the cartoon.
  a) Which details in the cartoon characterize how the people feel and what relationship they have?
  b) Were you surprised by what the young man said? What did you expect him to say?
  c) Do you consider the young man's proposal absurd/realistic/sensible?
  d) In groups of four, act out the conversation following the proposal.
- Can you imagine moving in with your boyfriend's/girlfriend's parents? Why, why not?

Reading and thinking ▸

1. a) What reasons are given for young adults staying with their parents?
   b) What problems do these families face?
   c) Why do the parents still put up with their children?
2. What makes the text humorous? What devices contribute to this effect? See page 121 for help.
3. a) What target group is this *column* aimed at?
   b) What reactions may it cause?

Column

Columns are regular contributions to a newspaper by the same person (columnist). They deal with topics of general interest in a personal, thought-provoking and often funny way.

Close-up: language ▸

1. The author makes use of various levels of speech (registers). See page 121.
   a) Form two teams. One team should look for the colloquial expressions or slang she uses, and the other should look for formal expressions. Find standard English expressions for them. (A good dictionary will help – see page 108.)
   b) Taking turns, each team should tell the members of the other team one of their expressions, who should then try to find a suitable standard expression for it. Compare this with what the team found who used the dictionary.
   c) Together, decide which expressions are worth being integrated into your active vocabulary.
2. What is the effect of this mix of levels?

A step further ▸

WB: p. 42, How to write a letter to the editor

- Write a news item that might have inspired the author to write her column. See the box on page 53 for help.
- Choose the perspective of one of the people mentioned in Katharine Whitehorn's column, and write a letter to the editor. See page 118 for help.
- Write a column on parents not letting their children go from the perspective of a young adult still living at home. Try to use some of the devices the author uses to make your text more enjoyable.
- Prepare and give a short talk (see page 107) on the following topic: "The parents' responsibility ends when their child comes of age. After that, society has to take over if the child needs help."

When you read this article for the first time, do not worry about understanding every word. Just try to understand the gist. The techniques described on page 108 will also help you to work out the meaning of unknown words.

Tell the birds about family life

The doves have got it about right, I reckon. They, alone among birds, give milk to their young. With both males and females using their beaks to feed the chicks, they can hardly be accused of being neglectful parents. But when they think that it has gone on long enough, they push the chicks off the perch. They then have to learn to fly before they hit the ground.

For about a month, they are not allowed back. Only after they prove they can survive on their own may they even fly with the flock, let alone return to the parental feed table.

No caring, educated, liberal parent would ever be so heartless; but I suspect a good many of us would like to be. Parents view with extreme gloom the new policy of some universities, which favour applicants who can live at home while they study. They also feel outraged by the suggestion that the scapegoat of our times – the single mother – should return to the parental nest, her child a charge on its unconsulted grandparents. Whatever happened to the idea that children grow up and leave home?

Unemployment happened, for a start; our lot could get a job if we tried, so our parents weren't likely to put up for long with us slothing round the house playing the piano. It's no good telling them to go and get a job if there isn't one. And even having a son or daughter in work by no means ensures that they will move out, with housing as tricky as it is. [...]

Money can be an extra irritant – and I don't just mean that the banks never seem to be open at times the young can get to them – they say. If you've got some, and they, through no fault of their own, haven't, it seems deeply mean not to subsidise them. Yet they hate the feeling of being dependent, so mostly what happens is 'loans'. There's a snare, too, in the working son or daughter who, quite correctly, offers to pay towards their keep. We've taken to refusing, and not from nobility; we've seen several relationships go sour because the one paying rent assumed he had rights: 'It's my home too.'

I can't say I've much to grumble about. I know an authoress who supports sons in their thirties, who only moan that she doesn't give them enough.

There's a professor whose daughter has not only moved back, but brings her boyfriend at weekends and has forced her mother to install a satellite dish to entertain him when she flags. And one family, who happily married off their daughter five years ago, now has her back because her husband decided that he never wanted marriage and all that – 'all that' being three very small children. [...]

It might be easier if there had always been a vast family around, but that isn't our culture: we are not tribal, we're supposed to fend for ourselves as individuals. For us, 'home is the place where, when you have to go there, they have to take you in'. It is not the place where you expect to be born, live out your life and die, as if you were a hereditary landowner. We can't be stretched on the rack to fit some ideal of an extended family; it doesn't exist.

But surely the pattern of grown-up sons and daughters staying with their parents until they marry, and indeed later, has been successfully around since time immemorial? Yes – but with a crucial difference. In a culture where everyone lives together all the time, it's the old who have the power.

'You can't have it both ways,' a scholar of India once mused to me. 'If you want the unending support and comfort of an extended family, you also have the interfering old ya-ya telling you what to do.' No modern parent has that sort of clout. We have brought up our children to expect too much equal treatment and – here's the irony – independence.

By Katharine Whitehorn, *The Observer,* 14 November, 1993.

21 **let alone** still less – 28 **gloom** unhappiness, despair – 38 **charge** *(formal) here:* s.o. one has to look after – 45 **our lot** *(informal) here:* our generation – 49 **to put up with s.th.** to tolerate s.th., to allow s.th. to happen – 69 **mean** *(double meaning)* unfair; unwilling to give money – 76 **to pay towards one's keep** to pay part of food costs, housing costs etc. – 78 **to take to s.th.** to start doing s.th. regularly – 103 **to flag** to start losing enthusiasm and energy – 116 **to fend for o.s.** to look after o.s. even in difficult situations – 124 **hereditary** [hɪ'redɪtrɪ] handed down from generation to generation – 126 **to stretch s.o. on the rack** centuries ago, a way of torturing s.o. – 127 **extended family** three or more generations of a family – 134 **since time immemorial** for longer than anyone can remember

Surviving without a dictionary

1 refers to *word family*
2 refers to *similar German, French or Latin words*
3 refers to *context*

8 **Dean Nolan** principal of Welton Academy
13 **roster** list of names
17 **virgin** *here:* young woman
21 **ye** [ji:] old form of "the" and "you"
21 **bud** flower just about to open
28 **to seize** *here:* to take hold of, to make the most of
32 **to snicker** to laugh quietly, without respect, usu. about s.th. thought dirty or rude

"Make your lives extraordinary"

- Describe the photo. What kind of situation does it show?
- Choose one of the following proverbs or quotations on time, and say why it appeals to you.
  Time flies.
  There's no time like the present.
  Life is short and time is swift.
  "I like the dreams of the future better than the memories of the past."
  (Jefferson)

▶ *N.H. Kleinbaum's novel* Dead Poets Society *is about a group of boys at Welton Academy, a private school in Vermont. A new English teacher, Mr Keating, has started working at the school and his rather unusual teaching methods surprise his class...*
The numbers given refer to the techniques described on page 108.

"Pick up your textbooks from the back, gentlemen, and let's retire[3] to the Honor Room."

Using the yardstick[2] as a pointer[1], Keating headed[3] to the door and walked out. The students sat, silent, not sure what to do.

"We'd better go with him," Neil said, leading the class to the back of the room. They each picked up a text, gathered their books, and proceeded[3] to the oak-paneled Welton Honor Room, where they had last waited to see Dean Nolan.

Keating walked around the room as the boys straggled in. He studied the walls, which were lined with class pictures dating back to the 1800s. Trophies[2] of every description filled shelves and glass cases.

Sensing that everyone was seated, Keating turned toward the class. "Mister" – Keating looked down at his roster – "Pitts," he said. "An unfortunate name. Stand up, Mister Pitts." Pitts stood. "Open your text, Pitts, to page 542 and read for us the first stanza of the poem," Keating instructed[1].

Pitts leafed[1] through his book. "To the Virgins, To Make Much of Time?" he asked.

"That's the one," Keating said, as the boys in the class chuckled out loud.

"Yes, sir," Pitts said. He cleared his throat.

"Gather ye rosebuds while ye may,
Old Time is still a-flying;
And this same flower that smiles today
Tomorrow will be dying."

He stopped. "Gather ye rosebuds while ye may," Keating repeated. "The Latin term for that sentiment is *Carpe Diem*. Does anyone know what that means?"

"Carpe Diem," Meeks, the Latin scholar, said. "Seize the day."

"Very good, Mr ...?"

"Meeks."

"Seize the day," Keating repeated. "Why does the poet write these lines?"

"Because he's in a hurry?" one student called out as the others snickered.

"No, No, No! It's because we're food for worms[2], lads!" Keating shouted. "Because we're only going to experience a limited[2] number of springs, summers, and falls[3]."

"One day, hard as it is to believe, each and every one of us is going to stop breathing, turn cold, and die!" He paused dramatically. "Stand up," he urged the students, "and peruse the faces of the boys who attended this school sixty or seventy years ago. Don't be timid[3]; go look at them."

The boys got up and walked to the class pictures lining the honor-room walls. They looked at faces of young men, staring out at them from the past.

"They're not that different than any of you, are they? Hope in their eyes, just like yours. They believe themselves destined[3] for wonderful things, just like many of you. Well, where are those smiles now, boys? What of the hope?"

The boys stared at the photos, their faces sober and reflective[2]. Keating walked swiftly around the room, pointing from photo to photo.

"Did most of them not wait until it was too late before making their lives into even one iota of what they were capable? In chasing the almighty deity of success, did they not squander their boyhood dreams? Most of those gentlemen are fertilizing daffodils now! However, if you get very close, boys, you can hear them whisper. Go ahead," he urged, "lean[2] in. Go on. Hear it? Can you?" The boys were quiet, some of them leaned hesitantly[1] toward the photographs. "Carpe Diem," Keating whispered loudly. "Seize the day. Make your lives extraordinary."

Todd, Neil, Knox, Charlie, Cameron, Meeks, Pitts, and the other boys all stared into the pictures on the walls, lost in thoughts that were rudely interrupted by the bell.

"Weird," Pitts said as he gathered up his books.

"But different," Neil said thoughtfully.

"Spooky[2]," Knox added, shivering slightly, as he headed out of the room.

"You think he'll test us on that stuff?" Cameron asked, looking confused.

"Oh, come on, Cameron," Charlie laughed, "don't you get anything?"

38 **to peruse** [pə'ru:z] *(formal)* to read; *here:* to look at carefully

46 **sober** *here:* serious, thoughtful

49 **iota** [aɪ'əʊtə] tiny amount

50 **deity** ['dəɪətɪ] *(formal)* god, goddess

51 **to fertilize daffodils** *(fig., humorous,)* to be food for flowers, i.e. to be dead

63 **to get s.th.** *(informal)* to understand s.th.

From *Dead Poets Society* by N.H. Kleinbaum, New York: Bantam Books, 1989, pp. 24–27.

◀ Reading and thinking

1. a) What tricks does Keating use to get his class interested in poetry?
   b) Describe the students' reaction.
2. Now read the complete poem "To the Virgins, to Make Much of Time" on page 74. Is Keating's interpretation in line with the complete poem? Read the box on page 75 and then find your answer in three steps:
   – Analyse the imagery (also see page 121) Herrick uses for the passing of time. What symbolic value do these images have?
   – Show how the individual stanzas are sense units in their own right and how they are logically connected.
   – Try out different ways of reading this poem aloud. Where does the natural rhythm go against the metre, and what effect does this have?
3. Keating's approach is quite unconventional, as he concentrates on his students rather than on the poem.
   a) Plan an extremely traditional lesson, concentrating on the poem as a piece of art rather than on the person reading it. Work in small groups or with a partner, and present your alternative to the class. See page 106.
   b) Discuss the advantages and disadvantages of both extremes.

Euphemism

A more gentle expression used instead of the more usual one to express unpleasant, frightening or embarrassing facts.

WB: p. 6, Grammar review; p. 12, Text quiz; p. 17, Vocabulary test

To the Virgins, to Make Much of Time

Gather ye rosebuds while ye may,
Old Time is still a-flying;
And this same flower that smiles today
Tomorrow will be dying.

The glorious lamp of heaven, the sun,
The higher he's a-getting,
The sooner will his race be run,
And nearer he's to setting.

That age is best which is the first,
When youth and blood are warmer;
But being spent, the worse, and worst
Times still succeed the former.

Then be not coy, but use your time,
And while ye may, go marry:
For having lost but once your prime,
You may for ever tarry.

By Robert Herrick (1591–1674)

13 **coy** being, or pretending to be, very shy
14 **to go marry** *(arch.)* to enjoy o.s.
15 **prime** best time of one's life
16 **to tarry** *(arch.)* to stay longer than one meant to

Here are two more poems on transience.

Vitae Summa Brevis Spem Nos Vetat Incohare Longam

They are not long, the weeping and the laughter,
Love and desire and hate:
I think they have no portion in us after
We pass the gate.

They are not long, the days of wine and roses:
Out of a misty dream
Our path emerges for a while, then closes
Within a dream.

By Ernest Dowson (1867–1900)

title: Life's short span forbids us to enter on far-reaching hopes. (Horace)

3 **to have a portion in** *here:* to be part of, to belong to

6 **misty** ⚠ foggy, unclear
7 **to emerge** [-'-] to appear

Salvador Dalí, *The Persistence of Memory,* 1931

What do you think Dalí is trying to say about the passing of time?

Ending

The love we thought would never stop
now cools like a congealing chop.
The kisses that were hot as curry
are bird-pecks taken in a hurry.
The hands that held electric charges
now lie inert as four moored barges.
The feet that ran to meet a date
are running slow and running late.
The eyes that shone and seldom shut
are victims of a power cut.
The parts that then transmitted joy
are now reserved and cold and coy.
Romance, expected once to stay,
has left a note saying GONE AWAY.

By Gavin Ewart (b. 1916)

2 **to congeal** [kən'dʒi:l] to thicken
2 **chop** piece of meat people eat, usually pork
4 **bird-peck** birds peck at things with their beaks
5 **charge** *here:* power in a battery
6 **inert** without moving
6 **moored barge** boat fastened to the land
11 **to transmit** to send out (as by radio waves)

Reading and comparing

1. Would you present one of the last two poems rather than Herrick's poem to a group of teenagers? Give reasons.
2. "Ending" has some features of a sonnet (see the definition on page 125). Which ones can you identify?
3. Say whether you think Ewart's poem is serious/mocking/old-fashioned/modern.

A step further

- Write a traditional or modern poem, finding your own symbols of how time passes. See page 118 of this book and WB: page 38 for help.

project

Compile your own class anthology.

1. Browse through poetry anthologies and choose poems that you find interesting. (You may want to include the lyrics of your favourite songs.)
2. Present them to the class, briefly giving reasons for your choice.
3. Together, decide which poems to include in your anthology.
4. Arrange them (e.g. according to topic, time of origin).
5. Decide on the layout (type of print, illustrations, annotations, etc.).
6. Copy the pages and put them in folders so you can keep adding poems.

Poetry

A *poem* is usually a fairly short piece of writing, divided into single lines. It often expresses the *speaker's* experiences.

Traditional poetry makes use of four very important *poetic devices:*

1. *metre:* the regular pattern of stressed and unstressed syllables.
2. *stanza:* usually regular number of lines which form a unit.
3. *rhyme:* similarity of sounds in two or more words. Words rhyme when their accented vowels and all following sounds are identical. This often occurs at the end of lines *(end rhyme)*. The pattern created is called a *rhyme scheme.* It is represented using small letters (see Herrick: abab cdcd…).
4. *rhythm:* the flow of language created by the arrangement of unstressed and stressed syllables. It is mainly based on metre.

Modern poetry often does not have a regular rhythm or a rhyme scheme.

Picking partners

Dear Mary…

Before you read ▶

- Most youth magazines run 'problem pages'. Find out the main problems they deal with, and categorize them.
- In English-speaking countries, the columnists answering the letters on the problem page are often called 'agony aunts'.
  a) Collect all the *connotations* evoked by this expression, and present them in a systematic way.
  b) Discuss whether the term is appreciative/derogatory/humorous/ironic.
- a) Why do people write to advice columnists?
  b) Why do people read problem pages?

Connotation
Associations and emotions a word may evoke.

Denotation
Literal meaning of a word.

WB: p. 13, Mistaken affections

"I didn't fancy him"

There is a boy in my class and we used to be good friends. We'd sit together and talk about all sorts of things. Then he told me that he loved me and wanted to go out with me. I didn't fancy him, so I said 'no' nicely, as I still wanted to stay friends with him. But since then he has been really horrible, telling people that I'm a bitch, and it really upsets me. I've tried to talk to him, but he ignores me. He's told everyone that I've treated him badly, but I just don't understand what I've done wrong. Sarah (15), London

7 **bitch** *(informal, rude)* unpleasant woman

Reading and imagining ▶

Imagine you were the advice columnist.

a) In class, discuss what aspects of the letter must be considered in the answer, and plan a letter of advice. Begin with a few words of reassurance. Then, pinpoint the problem, and analyse it if necessary. Give your advice in several steps that are easy to put into practice.
b) Write a letter of advice individually. Make sure it will be understood by a 15-year-old.
c) Compare your letters in class. How well is the problem dealt with? How well is the writer's personality considered in the answers? How seriously is she taken?

- Sarah telephones CHILDLINE, an organization of professionals and volunteers who answer children's distress calls all day round. With a partner, turn the letter and the answer you considered best into a telephone dialogue. Act the dialogue out, or present a tape recording to the class.
- Sarah puts the advice she has been given into practice.
  a) In groups, girls develop strategies of how to make the boy change his behaviour. Remember to anticipate a variety of possible reactions from the boy and how best to cope with them! Meanwhile, groups of boys develop a variety of possible reactions to Sarah.
  b) Members of each group act out the dialogue between Sarah and the boy.
  c) The rest of the class decides which dialogue was the most authentic one, and why.

Talking about relationships II

to be fond of s.o.
to be keen on s.o.
to have a crush on s.o.
to fancy s.o.
to fall in love with s.o.
to be (madly) in love with s.o.

to go on a date with s.o.
to have a date with s.o.
to go out with s.o.
to date s.o.

to split up with s.o.
to break up with s.o.

"She keeps falling madly in love"

We're worried about our friend. She keeps falling madly in love with famous actors and pop stars. She recently saw a guy in a film and has now spent hours watching it. She's put posters of him up everywhere and talks about him all the time. Then last week, she found out that he had recently married an actress and she was devastated. She started crying and now can't concentrate at school. What's happened to her? We want to help her, but don't know what to do.

Former "Take That" fans

For whatever reason, your friend keeps falling madly in love with men who are completely out of reach, but she tells herself that it might work out. She thinks to herself "if only I could meet him, then he'd like me, go out with me and fall in love with me". This is why she gets so upset when she finds out they've got someone else. As far as she is concerned, these fantasies are serious relationships. That's why she became so upset when she found out he had got married. The best thing you can do is to let her talk about her fantasies – but don't make fun of her. Remind her every now and then that they are not real. In time her infatuation should pass and she'll become interested in boys around her. However, if it continues or she starts to get seriously depressed then you should have a chat with her mum.

7 **devastated** extremely shocked and upset

By Mary Turvey

Reading and comparing

1. Compare the problem in the letter with the advice given.
   a) To what degree is the advice helpful?
   b) What would you change, and why?
2. Write your own answer to the letter individually. Compare the letters and decide on the version that you think should have been printed instead of the original one.

A step further

- Agony aunts are also found on the Internet.
  a) Think of questions that might be asked, and have the class answer them. You may want to compete for the most concise and at the same time original question and answer.
  b) Try to find an agony aunt on the Internet and send her some of your questions. Compare her answers with the ones you wrote down.
- An advice columnist in the hot seat.
  a) In groups, think of questions concerning the duties and possibilities of the job. One group, whose members will later play the role of the advice columnists, should think of details concerning their job description.
  b) Put each advice columnist in the hot seat, and ask them your questions.
  c) After the hot seat session, decide who represented his/her job best, and why.

Surviving adolescence

Before you listen ▶

- What typical teenage problems can you think of?
  Write down as many as you can think of in a minute. Then collect all your ideas on the board or on a transparency, arranging them as logically as possible.
- a) What do you think adults mean when calling an adolescent a 'typical teenage worrier'?
  b) Collect as many characteristics as possible to define the term. Then write a definition for a parents' guide to teenagers.

WB: p. 14, An abrupt ending

▶ *You are going to hear 16-year-old Niamh* [ni:v] *Yorke talking about adolescence. She talks about her insecurities, hang-ups and anxieties. Before you listen, read page 111 and then have a look at the following annotations:*

bout *here:* outbreak, attack
pathetic ⚠ arousing pity; *here:* stupid, weak
outcast s.o. not accepted by a group
moody depressed, unhappy
vain extremely proud of one's beauty

Listening for gist: finding key words ▶

While listening to Niamh for the first time, note down key words and phrases for the following:
a) what she was most concerned about when she was younger;
b) what she is most concerned about now.

Listening for detail: key words and beyond ▶

1. Listen to Niamh again, and add any details connected with your key words.
2. On the basis of your key words, discuss
   a) why Niamh criticizes the media, especially youth magazines;
   b) why she criticizes some of her female friends;
   c) what she may mean when she talks about "having an identity".

The photo shows an everyday situation. What sort of things might these girls be talking about? Using the phrases below and any you noted down while listening to Niamh and Danielle, write their dialogue. You may be funny if you like.

Teenage talk

It's a scream: *really funny*
It's a nightmare: *awful*
It's unreal: *really good*
It's cool: *okay*
mates: *friends*
to chill out: *to relax*
to hang out with s.o.: *to spend time with s.o.*

▶ *You are now going to hear 21-year-old Danielle Homburg talking about growing up.*
Read through the annotations below before you listen to her.

to detest [-'-] to dislike very much
to strive for s.th. to try very hard to reach s.th.
encounter short, often unexpected meeting
exploration *here:* trying to find out what s.th. is like
conquest ['--] *here:* s.o. whose love or admiration you have gained

◀ Listening for gist: developing a grid

1. Without taking notes, concentrate on the different sections of Danielle's life which she talks about.
2. Now draw a grid which indicates these sections. You might want to have another look at page 111 for help.

◀ Listening for detail: working with your grid

1. Listen again and add details to each section of your grid.
2. Describe the stages Danielle went through concerning relationships with boys.

◀ Listening and comparing

Listen to Niamh and Danielle again, this time concentrating on the way they talk about themselves and their experiences.

a) Which expressions show that Niamh is worried, which show that she is still confused?
b) Which expressions show that Danielle has outgrown her anxieties? What makes her statement sound humorous?

◀ A step further

- Danielle and Niamh meet in the cafeteria of the radio station after having recorded their statements. Danielle wants to know what exactly Niamh meant when saying she had "a lot of feminism", and Niamh cannot understand why Danielle is waiting for a man as a "reward for surviving adolescence". Make up their conversation in small groups, and present the dialogue to the class.
- Dealing with the same topics, write statements from a male teenager's/young man's point of view. Then discuss parallels and differences.

WB: pp. 28–29, From monologue to dialogue; pp. 45–46, How to hold a conversation 1/2

◀ project

Your partner school in Great Britain has been asked to make a radio programme (see page 122) on "Young women in Europe". They would like you to join in, informing British listeners on the German perspective. You are given about 15 minutes speaking time plus another 10 minutes for music.

1. Decide which topics you want to cover.
2. Decide how you want to present these topics: which of them would be best covered by spontaneous interviews, which by longer prepared statements? What background information will you give? What music would you like?
3. Plan the order of the interviews and statements, making sure it is varied.
4. Decide who is going to do what. Then prepare questions for interviews, gather background information, choose the music, etc. You will also need a team of sound engineers.
5. Conduct the interviews and record the statements.
6. Together, listen to the material and edit it.

WB: p. 12, Text quiz; p. 17, Vocabulary test

The River

Before you listen ▶

- a) Together, make a mind map on 'water' (see page 63).
  b) Pick out those aspects of the mind map that hint at the symbolic value of water, and choose one of them to write a fictitious dream or nightmare in which water plays a role.

First impressions ▶

1. Just listen to the song, trying to capture its mood. What effect do the melody, the singer's voice, the arrangement and the accompaniment of the song have?
2. Listen again, this time concentrating on the lyrics.
   a) Do you think the song is a typical love story? Why, why not?
   b) Do you think there can be a happy ending? Give reasons.

Talking about songs

The song is	relaxing • soothing • calming • moving
The lyrics are	sad • disturbing • melancholic
The mood is	aggressive • harsh • bitter

The song has…
a striking/pleasant/simple/catchy melody • a repeated chorus/refrain
a good/boring/repetitive bass line/beat • a complicated/simple rhythm

The lead singer has a deep/husky/grating/high-pitched voice

Listening, reading and enjoying ▶

1. What stages does the relationship go through?
2. Whose point of view is given, and how does this influence the listeners' attitude towards this love story?
3. What evidence is there that love has not died?
4. Analyse the refrain.
   a) What symbolic value does the river have?
   b) What is the function of the changes in the refrain?

Close-up: tenses ▶

Imagine Mary is trying to explain to a friend when and how things went wrong, as well as how she feels about the changes in her life. You might want to begin in the following way:
"We haven't seen each other lately. We got to know each other at high school…".

A step further ▶

- Add a stanza to give the song a happy ending.
- Rewrite the song from the woman's point of view, taking over as much as possible from the original.
- Change the song into a short story. You'll find some help on page 117 of this book and WB: pp. 34–35, "How to write a 'plot' story/'slice-of-life' story".

I come from down in the valley
Where mister, when you're young
They bring you up
To do like your daddy done
Me and Mary we met in high school
When she was just seventeen
We'd drive out of this valley
Down to where the fields were green

We'd go down to the river
And into the river we'd dive
Oh down to the river we'd ride

Then I got Mary pregnant
And, man, that was all she wrote
And for my nineteenth birthday
I got a union card and a wedding coat
We went down to the courthouse
And the judge put it all to rest
No wedding day smiles, no walk down the aisle,
No flowers, no wedding dress

That night we went down to the river
And into the river we'd dive
Oh down to the river we did ride

I got a job working construction
For the Johnstown Company
But lately there ain't been much work
On account of the economy
Now all them things that seemed so important
Well, mister they vanished right into the air
Now I just act like I don't remember
Mary acts like she don't care

But I remember us riding in my brother's car
Her body tan and wet down at the reservoir
At night on them banks I'd lie awake
And pull her close just to feel each breath she'd take
Now those memories come back to haunt me
They haunt me like a curse
Is a dream a lie if it don't come true
Or is it something worse, that sends me

Down to the river
Though I know the river is dry
That sends me down to the river tonight

Down to the river
My baby and I
Oh down to the river we ride

4 **done** *(informal)* has done
15 **to get a union card** *here:* to start working
16 **courthouse** *(AE)* building containing administrative offices of a county
17 **put it all to rest** married them
18 **aisle** [aɪl] passage between rows of seats in a church
25 **lately** ⚠ recently
25 **ain't** *(AE informal) here:* hasn't
29 **like** *(informal)* as if
30 **she don't** *(AE informal)* she doesn't
33 **on them** *(AE informal)* on those

By Bruce Springsteen

The black-haired girl

- a) Describe the photo from the cover of the novel *What's Eating Gilbert Grape*. Try to capture its mood.
  b) The photo is from the film based on the novel. Write a short scene into which it might fit. See "How to write a dramatic text" on page 117.

► *When you read the following extract from* "What's Eating Gilbert Grape" *you'll be able to guess the meaning of some words (marked with a 4) by saying them aloud. Don't forget to use the other techniques described on page 108 when you read this text!*

My sister Ellen works at the Dairy Dream. Some dream. They've got cones, colored sodas, candy bars, sprinkles, nuts, malts, shakes and one of those real dippy, sissy, piss-me-off bells that tinks[4] or clanks[4] or chimes when a person enters.

Before you enter the Dream, look in and study whatever girl is working. Make sure she doesn't see you, and then observe how she is hating her job. She wants to be in some fast car, you see, or home doing her nails – anywhere but in the Dream. Then push in the door, she'll hear the bell, and this smile will snap on like a zipper[4] unzipped. Or like God will take her face and turn it inside out. All of a sudden she'll be smiling like some beauty queen and so friendly and so interested and so happy. This is some shit, huh?

When I pull up at the Dairy Dream, I notice three girls. Two of them are chubby and plain and they are walking toward the Dream. They look familiar. The third girl doesn't. She is straddling a boys' bike, standing motionless, staring at something. The third girl my eyes can't deny.

She has black hair, thick and full. It drapes her shoulders. She has legs. Oh my. From where I'm sitting, she is not to be believed. She is the moon.

I put my truck in park, turn off the engine, take the headlights out, and roll down the window – all in slow motion. I breathe with great difficulty. Certain that I must be imagining this, I look around to see if this is Life that is happening. This is my truck. These are my hands. That's my little sister scraping the insides of the fudge machine. Yes, this is Life.

The other two girls go inside to order, but the one I'm aching for doesn't move. The bell clinks[4] or clanks[4] or dings[4], and one of them holds the door, thinking the girl on the bike is coming in. She's staring at something on the dirty white stucco wall of the Dream, however, and waves them off with a "No, thanks."

Now, Gilbert, get out of your truck now.

I remember my beer breath and find some Bazooka in my glove compartment and chew rapidly. I close my truck door slowly; my heart is pounding now, firing blood bullets. Minutes ago I was calm, a walking coma practically, and now, in seconds, I'm so glad to be alive. And so scared.

She's looking at some insects or maybe a spider. I move closer, trying to look at what she's looking at and trying not to look at her. I get close enough to smell her hair and make out the slope of her nose, the shape of her pillowlike lips. The round black glasses. The creamy skin, perfect skin.

I have seen God and he is this girl.

1 **dairy** foods such as milk, butter, eggs, etc.
2 **cone** *here:* pointed wafer for ice-cream
3 **dippy** *(informal)* crazy
3 **sissy** *(informal, rude)* too much like a girl
3 **piss-me-off** *(informal, rude)* extremely annoying

14 **familiar** ⚠ *here: opp. of* unknown
15 **my eyes can't deny** I can't keep my eyes off

23 **to ache for** to want very much (so much that it hurts)

Novel
A long fictional prose text. It often has a large number of characters, different settings and a complex plot.

I better say something fast. My mouth is drying out. As I step up behind her, she says, "Praying mantis. The male is sneaking up on the female. He wants to mate. If he's not careful, she'll turn around and bite off his head. His instinct will keep on mating. But when the rest of him is done, she'll eat what's left. That's how praying mantises mate. Interesting, huh? My name is Becky."

She turns, pulls down her glasses, and looks at me.

"Uh." is all I can say.

"I'm from Ann Arbor. My grandma lives here and I'm only here for that reason. My grandma's old, her hair is blue, and she'll die. Want to smoke?"

"No, thanks. I'm trying to quit."

"Really. Why?"

"Makes my skin gross? My teeth gross?"

"If you think it does, then I guess it does." She puts a cigarette between her perfect lips. "Smoking makes me feel alive. Helps me get through it. You know, the bullshit?"

I nod because I'll agree with anything she says. She lights her cigarette, looking like a magazine ad.

"You like me, don't you?"

"Yes."

"You think I'm beautiful."

I fight nodding but lose.

"I might be now, but one day I'll have blue hair and blotched skin and plastic teeth and maybe one breast left. If the thought of that appeals to you, then we might talk about hanging out. But if you're into the surface thing, the beauty thing, then I might just have to turn around, snap[4] off your head, and eat you."

I laugh but don't know why. This Becky girl doesn't even crack a smile. She goes inside and when that piss of a bell clinks or chimes, I fall back on the stucco of the Dairy Dream. I'm thinking, was the wind just knocked out of me or what?

It's then when I hear a soft crunch[4], a chomping of sorts. Turning, I see that the female mantis has caught the male, and his head has been snapped off. She is munching[4], he is squirming, and I run to my truck and drive out of there fast.

41 **to mate** to have sex
50 **gross** [grəus] ⚠ *here:* ugly

60 **blotched** spotted

62 **to hang out** *(informal) here:* to spend time together

67 **to knock the wind out of s.o.** *(informal, fig.)* to make s.o. feel faint, unable to breathe

From *What's Eating Gilbert Grape* by Peter Hedges, London: Mandarin Paperbacks, 1993, pp. 50–52.

Reading and thinking

1. What parts of the text make it clear that Gilbert is struck by 'love at first sight'? What similes and metaphors does he find for this?
2. What is Becky's definition of love? What do you think of this?
3. a) Find adjectives to characterize Becky and Gilbert.
   b) Now try to explain the reasons for their behaviour.
4. a) Which of the two do you sympathize with, and why?
   b) In what way is this influenced by the point of view?

WB: p. 29, Advice on chatting-up

A step further

- Rewrite this excerpt from the novel from Becky's (first-person) point of view.
- Do you think that Gilbert and Becky will "hang out"? Discuss this in class, giving reasons for your answer.

project

Turn the text into a film scene and film it. See page 123 for further help.

"Love stinks"

Before you read ▶

- Read the comic strip below. Then invent a suitable ending of your own for "Love is…".

to be through with s.o. *(informal)* to stop going out with s.o.

- a) Look at the list of proverbs on love. In pairs, choose the six proverbs you agree with most. Then get together with two other students, compare your opinions and try to agree on a list of five proverbs which you all find true. Repeat this with another group of four people and agree on your four favourite proverbs. At each stage of the discussion try to win the other students over to your side by explaining your views.
  b) Finally choose a spokesperson who should sum up your group's results for the rest of the class.

WB: p. 27, Expressing certainties

The first love is the fastest.
Love is just a four-letter word.
Love is blind.
Absence makes the heart grow fonder.
Marry late or never.
One cannot love and be wise.
Love will find a way.
Never rely on love or the weather.
'Tis better to have loved and lost than never to have loved at all.

Characters
GIRL
YOUTH

[The scene is an underground tube station, green tiled wall in the background sporting various advertisements using the theme of romantic love to sell. A GIRL *enters left, carrying a guitar in its case. She takes it from the case, proceeds to lay the case open in front of her, and fixes the instrument around her neck. She strums a few chords, tuning up the guitar. She then starts to sing, acknowledging a number of passers-by who throw coins into the case.]*

GIRL He'll tell you you're a poet
And he'll say you've got a mind
He'll tell you that your spirit is a dancer
But if you want to go where he don't want you to go
Don't take no for an answer
I used to fall for it

9 **to acknowledge** [ək'nɒlɪdʒ] *here:* to show one has seen s.o., e.g. by nodding

16 **to fall for s.th.** *(informal)* to be taken in by s.th., to believe s.th.

But now I think
Love stinks
Love stinks

[Enter a Youth, *right, who leans against the wall, watching the* Girl.*]*

Girl He's sittin' on a salary
He's sittin' pretty safe
He had the urge to roam but he ignored it
He says that young and free is the only way to be
But don't look at me, I can't afford it
I used to fall for it
But now I think
Love stinks
Love stinks [...]

*[*Girl *finishes the song with a flourish on the guitar, and* Youth *advances centre stage, still staring at her.]*

Youth That was a weird song. Where did you find it?

Girl I didn't find it, I wrote it.

Youth Oh, clever girl! But what's it supposed to be about?

Girl How can you say it's weird if you don't know what it's about?

Youth Well, love stinks. What's that supposed to mean?

Girl I would have thought it was self-explanatory. Love is a many-splendoured thing? What on earth does that mean?

Youth Yes, but love stinks! You can't really think that? Surely?

Girl Look you wouldn't be asking a bloke all these questions, would you? [...]

Youth I just thought we might ...

Girl Go for a drink.

Youth Yes. Go for a –

Girl Maybe a takeaway?

Youth Maybe a takea –

Girl Hold hands?

Youth Hold hands.

Girl Walk in the moonlight?

Youth Walk in the moon –

Girl Whisper sweet nuthins?

Youth Whisper sweet –

Girl Sense an ever-growing realisation that, at last, after years of longing for, searching for, yearning for, burning for love – that this is the real thing.

Youth Sense an ever –

Girl After one drink and a takeaway?

Youth Well, no it ...

Girl No, it wouldn't, would it? It seems that every love affair in the history of civilisation started off with a great big bang and went steadily downhill. Look at the trouble caused by love. Romeo and Juliet! Anthony and Cleopatra! Helen of Troy and Whatshisname!

Youth Little and Large?

Girl Little and – OK. Typical male. As soon as the talk gets serious, makes flippant remarks in an attempt to run away from it.

23 **to roam** *here:* to see the world, not to settle down

30 **flourish** ['flʌrɪʃ] *here:* especially impressive chord

37 **many-splendoured** *(poetic)* very wonderful

40 **bloke** *(BE informal)* man

51 **nuthins** = nothings
to whisper sweet nothings *(informal)* to whisper words of affection to each other (of lovers)

62 **Helen of Troy** figure from Greek mythology; the city of Troy was destroyed because of her

63 **Little and Large** two British comedians with a well-known TV show

65 **flippant** disrespectful, not serious

YOUTH It's not that. It's just that I hate depressing conversations. And I can't understand how you've managed to get so cynical. I mean, you're only young, but you sound like you've had a lifetime of *[Plays imaginary violin]* pain, disappointment, and heartbreak.

GIRL I've just heard too many people saying 'What are you doing tonight?'

YOUTH How do you see it then?

GIRL What?

YOUTH Our relationship developing?

GIRL I don't.

YOUTH Well, what's your scenario? Or what used to be your scenario before you got so bitter?

GIRL I'm not bitter. I simply see love as different from the way it's presented all the time. I don't want to marry someone thinking I'm in love and end up twenty years later detesting his entrails ... you know *[Sarcastically]* hating his guts ... When I say love stinks, I don't mean love stinks ... I mean romantic fiction love stinks ... soap opera love stinks ... front page of the *Sun*, nine-times married star says 'At last I've found Mr. Right', love stinks.

YOUTH What about love at first sight?

GIRL One night stand.

YOUTH Electric attraction?

GIRL Propinquity. *[To audience]* Look it up.

YOUTH Overwhelming desire?

GIRL Bad breath.

YOUTH A coming together of hearts and minds in a tumultuous collision?

GIRL Barbara Cartland.

YOUTH Engagement rings?

GIRL Ownership.

YOUTH Wedding bells?

GIRL Toll for thee.

YOUTH Honeymoon?

GIRL Air traffic controllers' strike.

YOUTH Buy first house?

GIRL Little box.

YOUTH Get new job?

GIRL Wage slave.

YOUTH Have two kids?

GIRL Who? You or me?

YOUTH Settle down?

GIRL Go to seed.

YOUTH Make new friends?

GIRL As boring as we are.

YOUTH Get promoted?

GIRL Suffer stress.

79 **entrails** = **guts** *Eingeweide*

80 **to hate s.o.'s guts** *(informal)* to hate s.o. very much

82 **the *Sun*** British tabloid newspaper

85 **one night stand** very brief affair, usu. limited to one night of sex

91 **Barbara Cartland** 'queen' of romantic female literature

92 **engagement** promise of marriage

95 **thee** old form of "you"

105 **to go to seed** *(informal, fig.)* to become run-down, to deteriorate

108 **to get promoted** to be given a better job and more money

From *Love Stinks* by Sue Hercombe and Pete Scott, in *Contemporary One-Act Plays, New Plays 3*, Oxford: Oxford University Press, 1989, pp. 24–29.

Reading and thinking

1. What attitudes towards love become clear during the conversation?
2. Form groups of males or females only.
   a) From the following list of adjectives, choose three that characterize the girl best and three that apply to the youth:
   friendly – arrogant – desperate – dominant – intrusive
   realistic – open-minded – persistent – romantic
   b) Compare your answers. Are there differences between the male and the female groups? If yes, what may have led to these disagreements?
3. Who do you think the protagonist is, and who is the *antagonist*?
4. a) What different kinds of information do the stage directions in the text provide?
   b) Following your recommendation, an English drama group thinks about performing this extract from a short play. Add some more stage directions to the text in order to make it clear how you would like to see it acted out.
5. Think back to "The black-haired girl" (pages 82–83). What do Becky and the girl on the one hand and Gilbert and the youth on the other hand have in common? Are these characteristics typical of today's youth or just clichés?

Antagonist
Character in a fictional text or drama who is opposed to, or in conflict with, the main character (protagonist).

Close-up: *if* clauses

Imagine you are asked to devise a multiple choice test for people who want to find out how good they are at making contact with others. Follow the example below and make up more questions, thinking of as many different situations and people as possible. In groups, girls should devise a test for boys, and boys a test for girls. Invent a point system and then write a key so that people know how good/bad they are at making contact with others. E.g.

1. If I saw an incredibly good-looking boy/girl at Piccadilly Circus studying a map of London,
   a) I would...
   b) ...
   c) ...
2. If ..., ...

project

In groups of three, prepare a radio version of the scene. What practical problems are you faced with? How might you solve them? See page 117 for help.

- Working in pairs of a girl and a boy, make up a satisfying ending for the text. You might want to refer to "Talking about relationships" on page 76.
- What do you think of the youth's chatting-up strategy? In pairs, think of an original chat-up line and act out the situation. Vote on the most convincing one: do males and females agree here?
- Write a paragraph supporting one of the following statements or give a short, provocative talk (see page 107 of this book and WB: p. 44, "How to prepare and give a talk") on one of them:
  "Modern young women are too assertive."
  "Young people expect too much from a partnership."
  "Romantic love is dead."
  "There are no real men any longer."

Would you use this photo in an advertisement "using the theme of romantic love to sell"? If yes, what sort of product would you advertise? If no, why not?

Finding one's place

I still haven't found what I'm looking for

Before you listen ▶

WB: p. 8, What has changed?

- What comes to your mind when somebody mentions 'pop songs'? Brainstorm with a partner for one minute, then briefly discuss your results in class.
- "The term 'pop culture' is a contradiction in terms. All pop is junk." Discuss.
- a) What do you expect a song with the title "I still haven't found what I'm looking for" to be about?
  b) Have you ever felt there is something you are looking for but haven't found? When?

First impressions ▶

Do not read the lyrics. Do not even try to understand them while first listening to the song. Just concentrate on the sound and the mood. In class, talk about your feelings, about what you like or do not like about the song. See page 80 for useful phrases for "Talking about songs".

I have climbed the highest mountains
I have run through the fields
Only to be with you
Only to be with you

I have run I have crawled
I have scaled these city walls
Only to be with you
But I still haven't found
What I'm looking for
But I still haven't found
What I'm looking for

I have kissed honey lips
Felt the healing in her fingertips
It burned like fire
This burning desire
I have spoke with the tongue of angels
I have held the hand of a devil
It was warm in the night
I was cold as a stone
But I still haven't found
What I'm looking for
But I still haven't found
What I'm looking for

I believe in the Kingdom Come
Then all the colours will bleed into one
But yes I'm still running
You broke the bonds
You loosed the chains
You carried the cross
And my shame
And my shame
You know I believe it
But I still haven't found
What I'm looking for
But I still haven't found
What I'm looking for

6 **to scale** to climb
16 **spoke** *(informal)* usu. spoken
24 **Kingdom Come** from the Lord's Prayer: "Thy Kingdom come"; heaven
25 **to bleed into one** to unite, like blood from different sources
28 **to loose chains** to loosen chains = to set free

Have you ever been to a concert like this? What sort of feelings did you (or might you) have?

Listening, reading and enjoying

1. a) Find out the different sections of the song, and give them headings.
   b) Identify the *semantic fields*. Which words belong to which field?
   c) Making use of your findings, say what the message of each section is. Compare what is similar and what is different about these sections.

Semantic fields
Groups of words referring to the same topic or phenomenon. A semantic field can include nouns, adjectives, verbs, phrases, idioms, etc. E.g. the semantic field "teaching and learning" might contain the following:

"Teaching and Learning"
lazy/diligent...
student/teacher/headteacher...
to study/to revise/to pass/to fail....
to take an exam/to set an exam...
The three R's: reading, writing, arithmetic...

2. To what degree can the speaker's various activities be taken *literally,* to what degree are they symbols or metaphors?
3. Interpret the title and the chorus on the basis of answers 1 and 2.
4. Who do you think "you" is?
5. Listen to the song again, remembering your first impressions. Do you feel differently about the song now that you have analysed the lyrics? Why, why not?

Literal
Using words in their everyday meaning.

Figurative
Using images and pictures that must be 'translated' to be understood.

Close-up: tenses

a) Identify the tenses and aspects most often used in this song.
b) Say in general what they are used for.
c) Explain why they are so dominant here.

A step further

- In groups, decide on a song you want to present to the class.
  a) Think of some activity to get the class interested in the topic of your song so that they will listen carefully.
  b) Say what you like about your song, then interpret it. Try to get the class involved as much as possible.
- a) Make up a questionnaire about the music tastes and habits of people you know. Conduct a survey, then present your findings to the class. See page 122 of this book and WB: page 43 for help.
  b) You could now do a similar survey with your partner school(s).
- "Today's pop junk is tomorrow's classic". Choose one of the following:
  a) Write an essay on this topic. See p. 116 of this book and WB: p. 31.
  b) Give a talk on this topic. See p. 107 of this book and WB: p. 44 for help.

project

Your school band is going to give a concert in your British partner school.
- Make posters and newspaper ads for this concert.
- Make a booklet about the band and the music they are going to play, to be sold at the concert.
- Write a newspaper article about the band for the local newspaper, to advertise the concert. See WB: p. 33 for help.
- Record a two-minute introduction of the band for the local British radio station.

WB: p. 12, Campaigning for improvements

Bitter sweet dreams

- a) What are your expectations when you look at this detail from a book cover?
  b) Write a one-page contribution (fictional or non-fictional) for a book in which young people talk about their past experiences and dreams of the future. Make it fun to read.
- a) You may have heard adults say, "I wouldn't want to be 18 nowadays!" What may they be thinking of?
  b) The same grown-ups may sigh: "I wish I were you!" Why?

Catherine Bull, *Littleover, Derby*
As I walk out of those gates I don't feel like laughing. I wonder what all my old friends will look like in twenty years' time. How many of the girls I knew who had high hopes and aspirations would end up unmarried mothers or drug addicts? I bet my gran didn't walk out of school wondering how many of her friends would be drug addicts. The unsheltered world outside those school gates seemed even worse than when I entered the school building at the beginning of my school career. My life has already been mapped out for the next two and a half years. I want to do the course but I am very apprehensive about it. I don't really know what to expect. I can't help wondering if all the hard work, all the revising and sitting stressful exams is all going to be worth it. There are so many people who are unemployed and not all of them have no qualifications. I hope that whatever else happens, I never have to turn to the dole queue.

Anonymous, *West Midlands*
I'm a teenager of eighteen. My teenage years haven't been as good as they could have been, they are over now in a way because I have a son; I'm an unmarried mother.

By the time my five-month-old son is capable of looking after himself I'll be thirty-four years old, too old to do things that I am now missing out on.

I would love to go to nightclubs and be like other people my age enjoying themselves: I'll never have these things but it's my own fault. I should have taken something to stop myself getting pregnant. […]

I got pregnant by my second boyfriend. He didn't want the baby but I wouldn't have an abortion. I was too scared. My boyfriend wouldn't marry me, he wanted to be free (these were the very words he said). He didn't want to listen to a screaming baby day in and day out. I got used to the idea after a while and I couldn't wait to put the clothes I'd bought on the baby; my boyfriend bought him nothing at all.

I never really thought about what it would be like to stay in every night while I was pregnant, I was so used to going out five nights a week. He's born now and I do love him, but I do wish that I was still free. Before I was pregnant I worked as a hairdresser. I hated the job at the time but

WB: p. 16, Being together/ In profile

12 **apprehensive** [--'--] nervous

16 **dole queue** [kju:] *(informal)* line of people without employment waiting to be given a job

now I think what a good job it was; I wish I could do it again. I'll never be a professional hairdresser now, it was something I always wanted to be. If I had the choice to go back in time I would and I'd make sure I didn't get pregnant this time. I would have a baby when I was married, but I'd want to be at least twenty-eight years old.

'Karina', *Potters Bar, Hertfordshire*
Being a teenager? I'm not sure I know what it means. Can't say I ever feel like one – more like a sort of 'intrusion' in life, you know – as if I don't belong. I think it can be nice or horrible but never ordinary. For me it's horrible. You know what the hardest thing about being a teenager is? Accepting yourself. Telling yourself, "Look, this is *you,* this is *your* body, *your* mind and you're stuck with it for the rest of your life, whether you like it or not." The second hardest thing is accepting others, accepting the world. I want to change things. I want to help the poor, I want to ban the bomb, I want us all to live in harmony, black, white, yellow, blue, whatever. I want to make my impression on the world, on this cold and bitter and confused place I live in. You see, I want to be remembered. [...]

You know, sometimes I get so depressed I could kill myself. But I never will. See, I want to change the world – God how feeble that sounds. When I was a kid, I wanted to be the first woman on the moon. Somebody beat me to it – c'est la vie! But now I feel it all slowly draining away from me: my ambition is seeping out of me, an ounce every month. But you have to have ambition. I despise all those neighbourhood girls I see at the cheese counter in Tesco's or at the checkout in Sainsbury's. Yes, I know, you're supposed to climb your way steadily up, reach the top of that social ladder of success. But when you finally arrive there, when you've made it after all those years of slog and sweat and tears, you're going to think to yourself – "was it worth it?"

Catherine Hiscock, *Maidstone, Kent*
Let's forget youthful poetic aspirations. They don't make the world go round. You've just finished having other people's creativity rammed down your throat for seven years and are masochistically about to do it again for another three years, of your own free will, feeling like a parasite on your father's wallet, and unlikely to have a highflying job to pay him back with. [...]

So you go out and look for a job, quite optimistically, because you've got millions of 'O' levels. Your name goes down on every file in town, you go to the Job Centre so often that it becomes a second home – and still no job. Your parents accept the fact that employers don't want temporary workers who could be leaving them in the lurch in October, and yet they still make it so clear they don't want an unemployed eighteen-year-old around that you consider joining the hippy peace convoy, rejecting society, parental rule, the 'system', and all creature comforts in favour of discovering your real self, eating burnt sausages and living in a bus with twenty other rather smelly people.

57 **to seep** *(fig.)* to flow very slowly

59 **Tesco's, Sainsbury's** names of big supermarket chains in GB

62 **slog** *(informal)* very hard work

66 **to ram s.th. down s.o.'s throat** *(informal)* to force s.o. to do s.th.

75 **to leave s.o. in the lurch** *(informal)* to fail to help s.o.

From *Bitter Sweet Dreams. Girls' and young women's own stories by the readers of Just Seventeen,* London: Virago Press Ltd., 1987.

Reading and reflecting

Talking about feelings

A person might feel…

apprehensive • bewildered • bitter • confused • curious • depressed • disappointed • doubtful • enthusiastic • flabbergasted • frustrated • fulfilled • happy • hopeful • horrified • insecure • light-hearted • lost • nervous • optimistic • pensive • pessimistic • relieved • sad • satisfied • scared • terrified • thoughtful • thrilled • troubled • uneasy • worried

1. Sum up the most important information of one of the four texts in no more than 50 words. See page 116 for help. Present your summary to the class.
2. Work in groups of four, each of you concentrating on one of the girls' texts.
   a) Study the girl's situation at the moment of writing. Find out about how she views the future, her hopes, anxieties, etc.
   b) Compare your findings.
   c) Finally, decide how you can present your findings to the class. See "How to present group work" on page 106.
3. a) Look up any of the words in the box on the left in your dictionary if you are not fully sure of the meaning (see page 108). Think of how you can arrange the words according to different criteria, which would help you to learn them more easily.
   b) Explain the way you have arranged the words to the class.
   c) Which of these adjectives applies best to the way one or more of the girls feel now that they have left school behind them? Support your answer with details from the texts. See "How to quote" on page 116.
4. Write a character profile of one of the four girls. You can draw a picture or find a suitable illustration, too. Explain and defend your profile (and picture or illustration) in class. See WB: p. 21, "Characters" for useful vocabulary.

Close-up: register

In groups, study the registers (see page 121) of the four texts.

a) Analyse the particular features of the language (e.g. vocabulary; phrases or idioms; rhetorical devices; syntax; tone; ...) used by the four girls.
b) Present your results in a systematic way and explain them to the other groups. See "How to present group work" on page 106.
c) Discuss to what degree these findings help you understand the four girls' characters.

Close-up: vocabulary

WB: p. 18, Understanding and learning new words, 3

The young women use a number of expressions worth integrating into your active vocabulary. For example: "to be capable of doing s.th." (l. 21), "to miss out on s.th." (l. 22), "to be used to doing s.th." (l. 33).
With a partner, go through the texts and add other words which you think it would be worth learning. Afterwards, explain your choice to the class.

A step further: creative writing

- Write one of the following:
  a) A short story based on one of the four texts. See page 117 for help.
  b) A drama scene involving one of the teenage writers and people close to her (a boy-friend; parents; a grandmother or a grandfather; etc.). See page 117 for help.
  c) A monologue between one of the teenage writers and her reflection in the mirror.
- Ten years later, the publishers of *Bitter Sweet Dreams* ask all the contributors to the book to write a sequel. Choose one of the girls and write her sequel.
- "Don't trust anyone over thirty!" Choose one of the following:
  a) Prepare a serious or humorous one-minute talk on this topic. See page 107 for further advice.
  b) Write an essay on it. See page 116 for help.

WB: p. 12, Text quiz; p. 13, Organizing a leaving party; p. 16, Help and advice

"Think for yourself"

Before you listen

- Look up what "volunteer" means in a dictionary. Then explain in class what your view of a "volunteer" is (character, reasons for becoming a volunteer, activities, ...).
- Talk about a community-orientated activity you or somebody you know took up voluntarily at some time or another.
- Look at the photo. What sort of situation does it show?

▸ *You are going to hear an interview with seventeen-year-old Holly Haynes, an American high school student. She talks about herself and the voluntary work she does.*
Before you begin, you should read through the following annotations:

to catch s.o. off guard to catch s.o. unprepared
errand short trip to do s.th. for s.o. else (e.g. shopping)
when push comes to shove *(informal)* when things become really difficult
Leave it to Beaver US television sitcom series

Preparing a checklist

What do you think the interviewer will ask her about? What would you ask her? What do you think she will stress in her answers? Write down a list of points, a 'checklist'. See page 111 for more help.

Listening for gist: using your checklist

1. Listen to the interview. Do not write anything down. Instead concentrate on:
   – the points on your list covered by the interview;
   – the points on your list not covered by the interview;
   – the points covered by the interview which are not on your list.
2. When you come to the end of the interview, correct your list. It would also be a good idea to re-arrange it so that it follows the course of the interview.

Listening for detail

Listen to the interview again and complete your list. You should also note down details about the individual points.

A step further

- On the basis of your checklist do one of the following:
  a) Prepare a talk called "Towards a better world – volunteers at work in the United States". If necessary, listen to the interview once again, to find out more details. See p. 107 of this book and WB: p. 44 for help.
  b) Write a news story with the headline, "One teenager who has found her place: Holly Haynes". You might want to refer to the box on page 53.
- Debate: "This House believes that young women should volunteer for a year after school (to balance the young men's year of military service)." See page 106 for help.

WB: p. 12, Text quiz; p. 12, Campaigning for improvements; p. 25, Associations

project

One of your classmates is an exchange student in the USA. He/She has been offered a ten-minute slot on the local radio station. His/Her topic is: "Voluntary work in Germany". He/She has asked the class for a finished tape. Make this tape in groups of four. See page 122 for further help.

You have the skills ... Oxfam can use them

Before you start

- In 1992, the George H. Gallup International Institute conducted a poll of American 13- to 17-year-olds to find out their attitudes towards materialism. They were asked how much they agreed with certain statements. The percent shows how many teenagers agreed with them very much.
  Making money is what it's all about. (25%)
  I want to help those less fortunate than myself. (58%)
  Personal happiness is more important than being rich. (67%)
  a) What do the findings say about the teenagers' goals? Do you agree with these statements?
  b) How can teenagers "help those less fortunate than (themselves)" and reach "personal happiness"? How does "personal happiness" relate to "making money"?
- If you were given an opportunity to work for an international organization like Greenpeace, Friends of the Earth, Care, the International Red Cross/Red Crescent, etc., would you accept? Give reasons.

Looking, reading and thinking

1. How does this advertisement try to catch and keep the reader's attention? Study the layout as well as the language. See pp. 57 and 115 for help.
2. Gather all the information on Oxfam that you can find in the advertisement. Using your findings, write a short encyclopedia entry.
3. In the business world, advertisers aim to produce desires and demands, i.e. they persuade consumers to buy what they would not necessarily buy of their own free will. To what degree does this apply to the Oxfam ad?

Talking about advertisements II

The advertisement/advert/ad...
addresses the target group directly...
refers to findings/surveys/statistics/other people's experiences...
is aimed at the readers' hearts not their heads...
aims to persuade the readers to...
appeals to readers who...
draws the readers' attention to...
makes readers curious about...

A step further

- Find an ad for a German organization or an international organization like Oxfam, and compare it with the Oxfam ad. Talk about the layout and the language, making use of the knowledge and techniques you acquired while studying the Oxfam ad.
- Imagine you are a representative of Oxfam, Care, or a similar organization. Give a talk (see page 107 of this book and/or WB: page 44), trying to persuade or convince your class that they should join. Make use of the rhetorical devices (see also page 121) typical of this kind of text.

WB: p. 12, Text quiz; p. 12, Campaigning for improvements; p. 25, Associations

project

European schools can set up partnerships with schools in other continents, including countries in the Third World. Where could you find out more about this? Read p. 122 "Gathering information" and then try to find information.

You have the skills...

'I initially joined Oxfam to give me something worthwhile to do while I was unemployed. I've since found a job but seven months later I am still enjoying my time as a volunteer. It gives me great satisfaction using my skills to help those less fortunate and it has shown me that there is much more to work than merely being paid for it!'
Andy Read,
Volunteer with
Bristol Oxfam
Group

THE WORLD IS FULL OF INJUSTICE. In developing countries a child dies from poverty every 2.4 seconds. In sub-Saharan Africa one quarter of all babies do not reach their first birthday. Tonight, one sixth of humanity will go to bed hungry. It doesn't have to be this way.

Oxfam is a partnership of people working for a fairer world. Your skills are needed.

Oxfam depends on volunteers. Without the hard work, enthusiasm and expertise of 27,000 volunteers throughout the UK and Ireland, Oxfam couldn't continue the fight against poverty and its causes.

By giving time – from a few hours a month to a full working week – you can help people challenge the exploitation and injustice which keeps them poor.

You have the skills – the poor of the developing world need them.

...Oxfam can use them

expertise ∇ *(formal)* [ekspəˈtiːz] special skill or knowledge based on experience – **to challenge** *here:* to start to fight against

Graham's story

Before you read

- a) "I'd rather my kids become happy dustmen than neurotic professors or business executives with ulcers."
  b) "If you're twenty and not a Leftist or Green, you've got no heart. If you're thirty and still a Leftist or Green, you've got no brains."
  Discuss these statements.
- Sometimes you find newspaper articles on people who have opted out. What might be the motivation of people who do this, and what kind of lifestyle may they want to choose?

I'm happier as a volunteer

Graham wanted to be an electronic engineer as a child. He went to public school and took four A-levels. Now aged 23, he has changed direction. He is a volunteer for Friends of the Earth in Sheffield and has "no firm plans" for the future.

When I was a kid I wanted to be an officer in the Royal Electricians Mechanical Engineers. My parents encouraged me. They wanted me to follow the fine examples set by the rest of the family. My father sent me to public school in Surrey. We were taught to be patriotic, right-wing, decent, hardworking citizens. Demonstrators, campaigners and unionists were people I looked upon with distaste. Hang all scroungers, I thought.

I left college with four A-levels and took a year out to travel. When the year finished I went on a three-month special leadership course with the Army, but already I was having second thoughts. Why should I put my life in danger just because my superior tells me to? For the next three years I did a degree in engineering and business studies. I graduated with a 2:1. But I didn't want to handle weapons or make multimillion-pound business decisions. The pollution and waste made me feel sick.

GRAHAM'S STORY

Instead I started working for Friends of the Earth in Sheffield. I got involved in a campaign about how government departments work and for the first time I saw what we were up against. The floodgates opened. I saw how badly the environment is treated. I became increasingly uncomfortable with the idea of supporting the Conservatives.

The Greens were very welcoming. I found them decent, open and honest. Whenever I had a problem they would go out of their way to help.

> My lifestyle is simple. There is no money for pleasure. I get up early, work all day.

My lifestyle is simple. I get up early, work all day and go to bed late. I'm at the environment centre most of the time – handing out information, working with the local radio station, putting packages together. I don't drink and I don't smoke, so I don't bother hanging out in pubs. I mix with my environmentally aware friends, then go home.

My bedsit is paid for by the government but it's not very nice. There's mould on the walls and the ceiling's on the verge of collapse. I get £36 a week dole. But there is nothing much left after buying food. I have to hitch-hike everywhere and there is no money for pleasure. I thought I'd cope with little money – I'm used to being a student after all. If I wasn't working for Friends of the Earth though, I'd go nuts.

But it's worth it. I am much happier with this lifestyle, happier as a volunteer. I decided that when my time comes I want to be able to look over my life and say: "This is what I've done to help the world."

My parents were unhappy about this change of mine. But they've mellowed out now – I wrote a long letter to them to explain. I just have to be careful about how I express my views to their friends.

I can't see myself going back to engineering although I miss it. I find myself wandering round the house picking up devices, looking at them, wondering why they have four ridges – how that might help them function. But the constraints of the industry stop me going back.

From *The Independent,* 26 January, 1995.

Reading and thinking

1. Work in pairs. One of you prepares 6 – 10 questions that can be answered from the text. The other one reads the text closely and tries to memorize as much of it as possible. Then the first student conducts an interview with Graham (the second student) for a TV youth programme. See page 107 for help.
2. To what degree is Graham's decision the result of his upbringing and education, to what degree has it been influenced by his surroundings?
3. Analyse the register (see page 121) and structure of this personal account. What does it tell you about the writer?
4. This autobiographical article has been taken from *The Independent,* a British daily paper.
   a) What sort of newspaper article is it? What elements in the text made you think so?
   b) What kind of readership is it aimed at?

A step further

- After finishing his studies, Graham goes home to tell his parents he is going to work for Friends of the Earth. They are disappointed as they hoped he would become an electronic engineer. In groups of three, plan your roles, write this scene, then act it out in class.
- After reading the newspaper article, one of the people Graham got in contact with in the course of his academic career (teacher or headmaster of the Surrey school; university professor; army instructor; etc.), writes Graham a letter. See page 118 of this book and/or WB: p. 40 for help.
- Graham is now applying for a job at an environmental consulting agency. Write his curriculum vitae. See page 118 for help.
- Let us imagine Graham continues this lifestyle for the rest of his life. What problems might arise? How might he be able to overcome them? Discuss in pairs, then present your answers to the class.

WB: p. 6, Grammar review; p. 12, Text quiz; p. 26, Word groups

"I used to be a pupil but I ran away to become a…" How would you continue this sentence? You may be funny if you like. Discuss your answers in class, giving reasons.

"I used to be an artist but I ran away to become a bank manager."

29 **superior** *here:* boss – 33 **to handle s.th.** ⚠ to deal with s.th.; *here:* to have to do with s.th. – 44 **to open the floodgates** *(fig.)* to set s.o.'s emotions free – 46 **uncomfortable** ⚠ not feeling good about s.th., uneasy – 50 **decent** ['--] ⚠ *here:* respectable – 52 **to go out of one's way to do s.th.** to take a lot of trouble to do s.th. – 68 **on the verge of** *(fig.)* close to, about to happen – 77 **to go nuts** *(informal)* to go crazy, mad – 86 **to mellow out** *(fig.) here:* to become kinder, more tolerant – 96 **ridge** *Kante*

Kid Stuff

The wise guys
tell me
that Christmas
is Kid Stuff …
Maybe they've got
something there –
Two thousand years ago
three wise guys
chased a star
across a continent
to bring
frankincense and myrrh
to a Kid
born in a manger
with an idea in his head …
And as the bombs
crash
all over the world today
the real wise guys know
that we've all got to go
chasing stars
again
in the hope
that we can get back
some of that
Kid Stuff
born two thousand years ago.

By Frank Horne, *Poetry Jump-Up*, comp. Grace Nickols, London: Puffin, 1990.

- What sort of picture would you choose to illustrate this poem?
- What activities do you think could help you understand the poem better, and enjoy it more?

Test yourself!

Introducing TOEFL, APIEL, IELTS and Cambridge

In the following pages you will have a chance to test your language skills. The theme of the texts "Asleep in class", "Working in the vineyards" and "I quit" is "Young people at work". The exercises which accompany the first two of these texts are based on some of the question formats used in international examinations such as TOEFL, APIEL, IELTS and Cambridge. These examinations are used by universities, in particular in Great Britain and the United States, to test students wishing to study in one of those countries. The aim of these tests is to make sure that potential students have a good level of English. As each university in Great Britain and the United States has its own admissions regulations for foreign students, it is a good idea to enquire about the exam(s) recognized and the score(s) expected by the university of your choice before you apply to them. In addition, certificates for international language examinations are well regarded by a growing number of employers all over the world.

What do these examinations look like?
- **TOEFL** (Test of English as a Foreign Language) is an American examination system which tests how well a student understands English. The test includes listening, reading, vocabulary, grammar and writing. Most of the exam is in a multiple choice format.
- **APIEL** (Advanced Placement International English Language), another American examination, is intended to test a student's ability to participate successfully in an English-language academic environment. In a three-hour exam, it tests reading, writing, listening and speaking.
- **IELTS** (International English Language Testing System) was designed by The British Council to test students who want to study at a university in countries such as Britain and Australia. The exam has four exam papers which test reading, writing, listening and speaking. The total exam time is approximately two-and-a-half hours.
- **Cambridge** The Cambridge First Certificate Examination (FCE), the Cambridge Advanced Examination in English (CAE) and the Cambridge Proficiency Examination in English (CPE) test the skills of reading, writing, use of English, listening and speaking.

You won't be planning to apply to a foreign university this year – if at all – but just to give you an idea of what the question types in the above exams are like, you could try the first two tests on pages 100–103. Then, you could write a similar set of exercises for the last text "I quit" on pages 104–105 and test your classmates! Good luck!

"Your overall TOEFL score is quite impressive. However, we'd like to have another look at your passport."

Chapter eight

Asleep in class

Read the text carefully and answer the questions that follow.

Charlotte Davis is anxious about A-level results. Not her own, but those of her pupils at Wallington High School for Girls, where she is deputy head. Davis believes 60 per cent of the girls will underachieve in their A-levels and GCSEs because they are working long hours in supermarkets, shoe shops and hairdressers.

Davis accuses the stores of exploiting pupils by encouraging them to work rather than study. She was horrified when Marks & Spencer asked a sixth-former at her school in Sutton, south London, to undertake a one-and-a-half-day induction course for a summer job the week before she sat the first part of her A-levels.

She ordered the girl – who had been offered extra tuition because her revision was "in a mess" – not to do the course and contacted M&S, charging it with being "immoral and irresponsible". M&S denied any coercion and said it wanted a highly educated workforce.

Other senior teachers, trade unions and children's organisations share Davis's concern. Teachers have told *The Observer* that supermarkets are routinely asking pupils for their timetables so they can be called on their mobile phones and asked to work during "free periods" – the time set aside for studying.

"These stores put pressure on the pupils at an age when they are often not strong enough to say No," said one headteacher in Manchester.

Many employers offer "double time" weekend work to school children rather than adult staff because they are cheaper and more malleable. Some offer pupils four-hour shifts – the maximum they can work before they have to be given a meal break.

The situation has worsened since the start of Sunday shopping and longer opening hours for shops during the week, acording to Davis. "Many of these children work long hours. They fall asleep in class and are unable to prepare properly for the most important exams in their lives."

2 **deputy head** *(BE) short for* **headmistress** second in command at the school

6 **to encourage s.o.** to motivate s.o. to do s.th.

9 **induction** introductory, *here:* training

13 **to charge s.o.** to accuse s.o.

14 **coercion** [kəʊ'ɜːʃn] making s.o. do s.th. by force

15 **trade union** organisation which defends workers' rights

22 **double time** double pay; paid for working at the weekend, etc.

24 **malleable** ['mælɪəbl] *(formal)* easily influenced

By David Harrison, *The Observer,* July 19, 1998.

Multiple choice ▶

Which of the possible answers given is correct?

1. According to the text, what is Charlotte Davis mainly concerned about?
   a) the pupils´ intellectual development
   b) the pupils´ physical well-being
   c) the wages pupils earn
   d) the pupils´ performance in school
2. In l. 10, the word "sat" is best interpreted to mean
   a) took
   b) tried
   c) passed
   d) practised
3. Why did Ms Davis order the girl not to do the M&S induction course?
   a) She hoped to teach the girl responsible behaviour.
   b) She did not want to support the girl´s laziness.
   c) She wanted to ensure the girl´s good grades.
   d) She feared the girl would fail in the exam.

4. According to the text, many teachers think pupils are exploited by the shops that employ them. The following examples are mentioned EXCEPT:
   a) paying low wages
   b) putting pressure on pupils
   c) making pupils work night shifts
   d) distracting pupils from their studies

◀ Working with a monolingual dictionary

1. *Find the meaning of the following terms in a dictionary. Then explain them by referring to the school system of your state.*
   a) A-level (l. 1) b) GCSEs (l. 4)
2. *Which dictionary meaning of the following words fits in with the context?*
   a) to exploit (l. 6) b) revision (l. 12) c) shift (l. 24)

◀ Comprehension

Answer the following questions using information from the text. Do not quote the text directly.

1. Why are stores so interested in having pupils work for them?
2. In what ways do stores try to encourage pupils to work for them?
3. How do teachers feel about the employment of pupils by stores?

◀ Grammar

Choose the answer that best fills in the blank.

1. Davis claimed that stores __________ students by encouraging them to miss classes.
   a) exploits b) had been exploited c) exploit d) were exploiting
2. Stores are not breaking the law ______________ pupils weekend work.
   a) by offer b) when offer c) by offering d) by
3. ___________________ pupils are endangering their own futures.
   a) By miss classes c) The more
   b) Missing classes means that d) Most
4. Pupils ______________ by the stores to work in their free periods.
   a) are ask b) can be asked c) can ask d) should be asked

Which underlined part of the sentence (A, B, C or D) should be changed to give a correct sentence?

a) Ms. Davis is <u>worried</u> (A) that pupils who <u>working</u> (B) in their free time are in <u>danger</u> (C) of <u>failing</u> (D) their exams.
b) Stores <u>like</u> (A) <u>to employ</u> (B) young people <u>rather than</u> (C) old people who are less flexible and not as likely <u>as</u> (D) to say yes.
c) Some pupils <u>are given</u> (A) <u>four hours shifts</u> (B) which is <u>the most</u> (C) they can work <u>before taking</u> (D) a meal break.

◀ Writing an essay

Do you agree or disagree with the following statement? Write a 40-minute essay in which you agree or disagree with the statement or qualify it.
"Young people still at school should not be allowed to work in their free time."

Working in the vineyards

Read the text below carefully and answer the questions that follow. Try to work out the context in which events take place. Make a note of key words relating to the context as you read.

The garage was worn out by the years. It had no windows. The walls, eaten by termites, strained to support the roof full of holes. The dirt floor, populated by earthworms, looked like a gray road map.

That night, by the light of a kerosene lamp, we unpacked and cleaned our new home. Roberto swept away the loose dirt, leaving the hard ground. Papá plugged the holes in the walls with old newspapers and tin can tops. Mamá fed my little brothers and sisters. Papá and Roberto then brought in the mattress and placed it in the far corner of the garage. "Mamá, you and the little ones sleep on the mattress. Roberto, Panchito, and I will sleep outside under the trees," Papá said.

Early next morning Mr. Sullivan showed us where his crop was, and after breakfast, Papá, Roberto, and I headed for the vineyard to pick.

Around nine o'clock the temperature had risen to almost one hundred degrees. I was completely soaked in sweat and my mouth felt as if I had been chewing on a handkerchief. I walked over to the end of the row, picked up the jug of water we had brought, and began drinking. "Don't drink too much; you'll get sick," Roberto shouted. No sooner had he said that than I felt sick to my stomach. I dropped to my knees and let the jug roll off my hands. I remained motionless with my eyes glued on the hot sandy ground. All I could hear was the drone of insects. Slowly I began to recover. I poured water over my face and neck and watched the dirty water run down my arms to the ground.

I still felt a little dizzy when we took a break to eat lunch. It was past two o'clock and we sat underneath a large walnut tree that was on the side of the road. While we ate, Papá jotted down the number of boxes we had picked. Roberto drew designs on the ground with a stick. Suddenly I noticed Papá's face turn pale as he looked down the road. "Here comes the school bus," he whispered loudly in alarm. Instinctively, Roberto and I ran and hid in the vineyards. We did not want to get in trouble for not going to school. The neatly dressed boys about my age got off. They carried books under their arms. After they crossed the street, the bus drove away. Roberto and I came out from hiding and joined Papá. "*Tienen que tener cuidado*," he warned us.

2 **a dirt floor** a floor of hard earth

14 **one hundred degrees** i.e. Fahrenheit; approximately 38 degrees Celsius

25 **to jot down** to write down quickly

33 ***Tienen que…*** *(South America)* You have got to be careful

From *The Circuit – Stories from the life of a migrant child* by Francisco Jiménez, Albuquerque: University of New Mexico Press, 1997, pp. 77–79.

Multiple choice ▶

Which of the possible answers given is correct?

1. The family
   a) has always lived in the garage.
   b) owns the garage.
   c) has been employed to clean the garage.
   d) is living in the garage while they are working in the vineyard.
2. Mr. Sullivan
   a) works in the vineyard.
   b) owns the vineyard.

c) lives in the garage.
d) built the garage for the family to live in.

3. Panchito
   a) is weak and sick.
   b) sometimes becomes dizzy for no reason.
   c) finds the work in hot weather difficult.
   d) chews on a handkerchief when he is thirsty.
4. The boys on the bus
   a) are on their way to school.
   b) are coming home from school.
   c) are going to work when they get home.
   d) are looking for Panchito and Roberto.
5. *The following information is mentioned in the text EXCEPT:*
   a) Panchito's father does not want him and Roberto to go to school.
   b) Roberto and Panchito should go to school.
   c) Panchito's father needs the boys' help.
   d) It would be possible for the boys to go to school.

◀ Grammar

Choose the answer that best fills in the blank.

1. Roberto told Panchito ________________ too much.
   a) not drink b) to not drink c) to drink d) not to drink
2. The garage walls ______________ by termites before the family moved in.
   a) had eaten b) had been eaten c) was eaten d) became eaten
3. The two boys could get into trouble ________________ school.
   a) from missing b) in missing c) because of missing d) by missing

Which underlined part of the sentence (A, B, C or D) should be changed to give a correct sentence?

1. Papá told his wife and <u>youngest children</u> (A) <u>to take</u> (B) the mattress and he and the older boys <u>will go</u> (C) outside and <u>sleep</u> (D) under the trees.
2. <u>After working</u> (A) for a few hours the temperature was <u>so hot</u> (B) that Panchito <u>had a terrible thirst</u> (C) and <u>badly</u> (D) needed a drink.

◀ Writing a report

Panchito is a <u>poor</u> <u>migrant worker</u> <u>from Mexico</u> who has come to California with his family. Collect the words and phrases in the text which support the underlined words.

Now, imagine you are a social worker who visits the family. Using the words you collected above write a report for the local school board in which you describe:

– the family's situation and living conditions
– the reasons why Panchito and Roberto do not attend school
– the kind of work Panchito and Roberto do
– possible suggestions as to how their situation could be improved.

"I quit"

Now, you can take over the class! Read through the following text and decide what kind of exercises you would like to set for your classmates. You could include:

- *comprehension questions. Think of questions with who-what-when-where-why-which-how or you could make up multiple choice questions where only one answer is correct…*
- *grammar/vocabulary exercises. Rewrite sentences from the text incorrectly, your classmates should correct them with their books closed; choose words from the text and let your classmates find words with similar meanings…*
- *creative writing. Your classmates write a text describing the situation from someone else's point of view, suggest how the story began/continues…*

You could work out a marking scheme for the questions you have made up. Decide which mark corresponds to: excellent – good – average – fair – poor. Write down the answers to the questions, where possible, so that the person who does your exam can check his/her results.

In the following extract from John Updike's short story "A & P" the narrator, Sammy, is working in one of the chain of A & P supermarkets one summer. This particular day Sammy has been watching three girls, the leader of whom he privately calls Queenie, walking around the aisles.

1 **to haggle** to argue over a price
1 **lot** parking area
3 **dreary** uninteresting
6 **to blush** to go red
14 **superintendent** s.o. who manages and controls what others do
15 **plump** ⚠ fat
15 **plaid** [æ] square-patterned
16 **can** *(AE slang)* backside
16 **to pipe up** *(informal)* to begin to speak, esp. suddenly
22 **sore** *here AE:* angry, upset
23 **crummy** *(informal) here:* lower class

Lengel comes in from haggling with a truck full of cabbages on the lot and is about to scuttle into that door marked MANAGER behind which he hides all day when the girls touch his eye. Lengel's pretty dreary, teaches Sunday school and the rest, but he doesn't miss that much. He comes over and says, "Girls, this isn't the beach."

Queenie blushes, though maybe it's just a brush of sunburn I was noticing for the first time, now that she was so close. "My mother asked me to pick up a jar of herring snacks." […]

"That's all right," Lengel said. "But this isn't the beach." His repeating this struck me as funny, as if it had just occured to him, and he had been thinking all these years the A & P was a great big sand dune and he was the head lifeguard. He didn't like my smiling – as I say he doesn't miss much – but he concentrates on giving the girls that sad Sunday-school-superintendent stare.

Queenie's blush is no sunburn now, and the plump one in plaid, that I liked better from the back – a really sweet can – pipes up, "We weren't doing any shopping. We just came in for the one thing."

"That makes no difference," Lengel tells her, and I could see from the way his eyes went that he hadn't noticed she was wearing a two-piece before. "We want you decently dressed when you come in here."

"We *are* decent," Queenie says suddenly, her lower lip pushing, getting sore now that she remembers her place, a place from which the crowd that runs the A & P must look pretty crummy. Fancy Herring Snacks flashed in her very blue eyes.

"Girls, I don't want to argue with you. After this come in here with your shoulders covered. It's our policy." He turns his back. That's policy for you. Policy is what the kingpins want. What the others want is juvenile delinquency.

All this while, the customers had been showing up with their carts but, you know, sheep, seeing a scene, they had all bunched up on Stokesie, who shook open a paper bag as gently as peeling a peach, not wanting to miss a word. I could feel in the silence everybody getting nervous, most of all Lengel, who asks me, "Sammy, have you rung up their purchase?"

I thought and said "No" but it wasn't about that I was thinking. I go through the punches, 4, 9, GROC, TOT – it's more complicated than you think, and after you do it often enough, it begins to make a little song, that you hear words to, in my case "Hello *(bing)* there, you *(gung)* hap-py *pee*-pul *(splat)*!" – the *splat* being the drawer flying out. I uncrease the bill, tenderly as you may imagine [...] and pass a half and a penny into her narrow pink palm, and nestle the herrings in a bag and twist its neck and hand it over, all the time thinking.

The girls, and who'd blame them, are in a hurry to get out, so I say "I quit" to Lengel quick enough for them to hear, hoping they'll stop and watch me, their unsuspected hero. They keep right on going, into the electric eye; the door flies open and they flicker across the lot to their car, Queenie and Plaid and Big Tall Goony-Goony (not that as raw material she was so bad), leaving me with Lengel and a kink in his eyebrow.

"Did you say something, Sammy?"

"I said I quit."

"I thought you did."

"You didn't have to embarrass them."

"It was they who were embarrassing us."

I started to say something that came out "Fiddle-de-doo." It's a saying of my grandmother's, and I know she would have been pleased.

"I don't think you know what you're saying," Lengel said.

"I know you don't," I said. "But I do." I pull the bow at the back of my apron and start shrugging it off my shoulders. A couple customers that had been heading for my slot begin to knock against each other, like scared pigs in a chute.

Lengel sighs and begins to look very patient and old and gray. He's been a friend of my parents for years. "Sammy, you don't want to do this to your Mom and Dad," he tells me. It's true, I don't. But it seems to me that once you begin a gesture it's fatal not to go through with it. [...]

27 **kingpin** *(informal)* most important person, boss
28 **juvenile delinquency** crimes committed by young people
30 **to bunch up** to group together
31 **Stokesie** the narrator's colleague
36 **GROC** groceries
36 **TOT** sum total
39 **to uncrease** [s] to unfold, flatten out
41 **palm** [pɑːm] the flat part of the inside of the hand
47 **goon** a stupid person; **Goony** a grotesque comic-strip character
48 **kink** twist or bend
55 **Fiddle-de-doo** nonsense
61 **chute** a channel that transports things downwards

From "A&P" by John Updike, *Pigeon Feathers & Other Stories*, New York: Alfred A. Knopf Inc. 1962.

Speaking

Discussions: leading a discussion

As discussions should progress in an orderly way, the role of the discussion leader is very important. He/she should:

- Open the discussion with some kind of introduction.
- Make a note of participants who show that they wish to say something (e.g. by raising their hands), then give them an opportunity to speak.
- Bring in participants whom he/she feels have something to say but are too shy to put up their hands.
- Politely interrupt those who are monopolizing the discussion.
- Make sure that only one person speaks at one time.
- Sometimes summarize what has been said up to that point and at the end of the discussion (which does not have to arrive at a final conclusion!).
- Thank everybody for their contributions.

Discussions: panel discussions

In a panel discussion a small group of people discuss a subject in public, often on the radio. Some basic rules should be observed:

1. Choose a discussion leader. He/she should introduce the participants to the listeners/audience and decide whose turn it is to speak. Also see above.
2. The participants may
   – voice their own opinions, or
   – take over certain identities and roles.

   They may also take notes beforehand.

How to conduct a debate

A debate is a very formal discussion and has fixed procedures. The participants are as follows:

- chairperson whose role it is to see that the debate is carried out fairly and that proper debate procedure is observed;
- team for the motion (first and second speakers);
- team against the motion (first and second speakers);
- (audience).

1. First comes the motion or proposition, which is introduced by the chairperson. It usually begins with the words "This House believes that…".
2. Then the two teams give speeches, taking turns:
   – The motion is first of all proposed (put forward) by the first speaker for the motion.
   – The first speaker in the team against the motion then gives his/her rebuttal, i.e. answering speech.
   – The second speaker for the motion then gives a shorter speech.
   – Finally the second speaker against the motion gives his/her rebuttal.
3. Once all the speeches have been given, the debate is open to the floor (i.e. people in the audience may give their opinions).
4. The chairperson might then ask the first speakers to sum up his/her points, which is done very quickly.
5. Following this, the chairperson asks the audience to vote for or against the motion, or to abstain (i.e. to say they do not wish to vote for a particular side). The winning team is the one which gets the most votes. If both teams get the same number of votes, the chairperson is allowed to give his/her casting vote.

How to present group work

- Before you begin, decide who is going to do what, to avoid confusion during the presentation. If possible, everyone should be involved in some way.
- Make sure that your presentation is well-structured and easy to follow. If you are giving a longer presentation, use legible transparencies or hand out copies outlining the main points.
- Whatever material you are presenting, make sure it is easy to understand as well as interesting to look at.
- Don't interrupt each other. If one member of the group forgets to mention something, wait until he/she has finished speaking and then remind him/her. However, if someone seems to have forgotten what to say, or has a 'blackout', one of you should give him/her a little help.

How to conduct an interview

- Make sure your questions are clear. Avoid asking confusing questions and ones that can only be answered with 'yes' or 'no'.
- If you ask several people the same questions, always use the same wording. It also helps if you learn the questions by heart because this makes it easier to combine the results.
- Practise interviewing people so you get used to using the recorder automatically while concentrating on your partner. Do not practise with your real interviewees – too much spontaneity is lost if they have to give the same interview twice.
- Always allow time to get to know the person you are interviewing. Talk to your partner casually, informing him/her about the reason for the interview, etc. – until he/she feels relaxed.
- You should not interrupt your interviewee unless he/she really goes off the point (unimportant passages can always be cut out later). However, you may ask more detailed questions if you feel that he/she has some interesting things to say about a particular point.
- And of course – be friendly, look at your interviewee rather than at the counter on your tape recorder!

Note: If you sit rather than stand when conducting an interview, it may help both of you to relax.

How to prepare a short (one-minute) talk

In a lot of situations you are expected to give an explanation, take a position, or argue for or against something on the spot. Normally, you will only have a few moments to make up a response. If, however, you have to give a short prepared talk, you will need to do some work beforehand. Here are some suggestions that will help you to give a convincing, short (one-minute) talk.

Practising your talk

- Take three minutes to write down single words or phrases that represent central ideas/aspects (do not collect more than five words or phrases).
- Put the words/phrases into a logical order.

WB: page 44

- You should practise your talk first. Try to speak as fluently as possible.
- Keep an eye on your notes.
- Record your talk on a cassette. Then, listen to it and try to identify passages that need improvement.
- Then, repeat your talk.
- As you get better at preparing – and giving talks – reduce preparation time from three minutes to half a minute. Also try to keep the key words in mind, do not write them down any longer.

How to give a short (one-minute) talk

- Before you start, listen carefully to the question or prompt so you know exactly what to talk about.
- Think of key words and put them into a logical order.
- State the topic clearly in your first sentence.
- Briefly describe the situation or explain the issue. If you are talking about a controversial, subject you could:
  - offer arguments against and for the issue;
  - consider positions contrary to the one you are taking and then explain your own position.

WB: page 44

- Make sure that the point you want to make or the position you want to take is mentioned precisely and emphasized in the last sentence(s) of your talk.
- Remember to link your sentences and ideas (see page 119); this will help your audience to understand the logical order of your thoughts more easily.
- If you are speaking about a complicated topic, give the audience a brief outline of your talk. First, tell them briefly what you are going to say; second, say it; at the end, sum up for them what you have said.

Reading

How to use an English-English dictionary

This type of dictionary is monolingual. It usually gives you: the forms of the entry word; the word class (noun, verb, etc.); the pronunciation; the different meanings.
An English dictionary is very useful for you as a learner.
a) It gives you grammatical information: whether the verb takes an object, whether a noun is countable, etc.
b) It tells you how to use a word in context by giving example sentences and words with which it is often used (prepositions, idioms, etc.).
It is important to read the additional information – it will help you to avoid mistakes!

Note: Before you look up a word in your dictionary, check which word class it belongs to. This will help you to find its meaning more easily in the dictionary, e.g. if it is a noun, you needn't read the entries for the verb. (In some dictionaries the word class is given after the entry word or phonetics, and not in a separate column.)

The dictionary entry on the opposite page is taken from the *Collins Cobuild New English Learner's Dictionary.* After you have read through it, look up the entry for *cross* in your dictionary to see how it is explained.

How to use a bilingual dictionary

At first sight this type of dictionary might appeal to you more and it is certainly helpful if you just want to understand the meaning of a word. If, however, you want to use the word actively, here are two tips for you:

1. The first translation is not always the correct one, so read all the translations and choose the one that fits your context best.
2. If you use a German-English dictionary, look up the translation word in your English dictionary, too! This will not only help you to make sure that your word is the correct one, but you can also see how it is used in context by studying example sentences, set expressions, prepositions that follow it, etc.

How to survive without a dictionary

WB: pages 18–20

When you read texts in English you will sometimes come across words that are new to you. You can find out the meaning of some of these words without a dictionary, as you can often guess it from:

1. The **word family** by identifying the root word, prefixes, suffixes *(dis/agree/ment)* or the different elements of a compound *(word/play).*
2. Similar **German, French or Latin** words and expressions, e.g. *thorn* – Dorn; *phase* – Phase.
3. The **context** by looking at the words or sentences before and after the unknown word.
4. The **sound** by speaking the word aloud, e.g. *snap; ding.* These words have elements of onomatopoeia.

You will sometimes read a text and not be able to guess the meaning of certain words. But you should ask yourself if you really need to know the meaning to understand the gist. Try to read over the difficult word – you will often see that the general meaning of the sentence still becomes clear.
Finally, your common sense and general knowledge will also help you to guess the meaning of certain words.

How to write a book review

A review aims to give potential readers an accurate idea of a book, and to tell them why they should or should not read it. In your review you should include:

- a concise summary of the plot;
- the message, the characters and their relationships, the level of language, the form/structure of the book;
- your personal response (reactions, thoughts, etc.);
- the book's appeal, i.e. why it is good reading.

You could mention book length, information on the author, and the target audience the book is aimed at.

This is how you could proceed:

1. Read the book carefully, taking notes on content, characters, form and language.
2. Decide what aspects you want to concentrate on in your review.
3. Arrange your material so that you can later develop a train of thought that readers can follow easily.
4. Find an opening sentence that arouses interest.
5. Write a first draft of your review and check it for content, language, development of ideas and length.

6. Write an improved version, correcting any mistakes.
7. Reread your text and decide if this is the final version.
8. Scan your final version for mistakes before you present it to the class or hand it in to the teacher.

---

entry word (first word of the entry)

pronunciation

forms and spelling of the headword

1 – 14: different uses of *cross* with explanations

examples chosen to show typical contexts, grammatical structures, etc.

15: further uses of *cross* in other expressions, with cross-references to other entries

cross 1 verb and noun uses

cross /krɒs, AM krɔːs/ **crosses, crossing, crossed.** ◆◆◆◆◇ **1** If you **cross** something such as a room, road, or area of land, you move to the other side of it. If you **cross** to a place, you move over a room, road, or area in order to reach that place. *Nine Albanians have crossed the border into Greece... Egan crossed to the drinks cabinet and poured a Scotch.* VERB Vn V to/into n
2 A road, railway, or bridge that **crosses** an area of land or water passes over it. *The Defford to Eckington road crosses the river.* VERB Vn
3 When lines or roads **cross**, they meet and go across each other. *...where the pilgrimage route crosses the road to Quimper.* V-RECIP: pl-n V Vn
4 If someone or something **crosses** a limit or boundary, for example the limit of acceptable behaviour, they go beyond it. *When prep-school students buy cocaine to sell to their classmates, they have crossed the line from pranks to delinquency.* VERB Vn
5 If an expression **crosses** your face, it appears there briefly. *A mischievous look crosses his face.* VERB Vn WRITTEN
6 A **cross** is a shape or object that consists of a vertical line or piece with a shorter horizontal line or piece across it. See picture headed **shapes.** *...a cross on a silver chain.* N-COUNT
7 If Christians **cross** themselves, they make the sign of a cross by moving their hand across the top half of their body. VERB: V pron-refl
8 If you **cross** your arms, legs, or fingers, you put one of them on top of the other. *He was sitting there in the living room with his legs crossed.* VERB: Vn V-ed
9 A **cross** is a written mark in the shape of an X. You can use it, for example, to indicate that an answer to a question is wrong, to mark the position of something on a map, or to indicate your vote on a ballot paper. N-COUNT
10 If a cheque **is crossed**, two parallel lines are drawn across it to indicate that it must be paid into a bank account and cannot be cashed. *Postal orders should be crossed and made payable to Newmarket Promotions.* VB: usu passive be V-ed BRITISH
11 If you describe something as a **cross** that someone has to bear, you mean it is a problem or disadvantage which they have to deal with or endure. *My wife is much cleverer than me; it is a cross I have to bear.* N-COUNT
12 If you dare to **cross** someone who is likely to get angry, you dare to oppose them or refuse to do what they want. *If you ever cross him, forget it, you're finished.* VERB Vn
13 Something that is **a cross between** two things is neither one thing nor the other, but a mixture of both. *'Ha!' It was a cross between a laugh and a bark.* N-SING: a N between pl-n
14 In sports such as football and hockey, a **cross** is the passing of the ball from the side of the field to a player in the centre, usually in front of the goal. N-COUNT
15 See also **crossing.** • to **cross** your **fingers**: see **finger.** • **cross** my **heart**: see **heart.** • to **cross** your **mind**: see **mind.** • people's **paths cross**: see **path.** • to **cross swords**: see **sword.**

cross off. If you **cross off** a word on a list, you draw a line through it, because you have decided that it no longer belongs on the list. *They have enough trouble finding nutritious food without crossing meat off their shopping lists.* PHRASAL VB V P noun V n P n Also V n P

cross out. If you **cross out** words on a page, you draw a line through them, because they are wrong or because you want to change them. *He crossed out 'fellow subjects', and instead inserted 'fellow citizens'.* PHRASAL VB V P noun Also V n P

cross 2 adjective use

cross /krɒs, AM krɔːs/ **crosser, crossest.** ◆◆◇◇◇ Someone who is **cross** is rather angry or irritated. *I'm terribly cross with him.* ADJ-GRADED ♦ **cross·ly** *'No, no, no,' Morris said crossly.* ADV-GRADED: ADV with v

information about the frequency of the word (based on how often it occurs in the texts used for this dictionary)

word class: verb

Vn = verb + noun, i.e. verb is transitive
the verb is used with to/into and a noun

verb is reciprocal, i.e. shows a process in which 2 or more people or things interact with each other
plural noun + verb: explanation of reciprocal.

expression is used in written English more than in spoken English

the noun is countable

verb needs a reflexive pronoun in this usage

verb usually passive
be + V-ed, i.e. *to be crossed:* information about phrase

British English usage

noun is always singular
a + N + between, i.e. *a cross between:* information about phrase

phrasal verb
verb + particle + noun also verb + noun + particle (+ noun); i.e. *to cross off s.th. / to cross s.th off (a list)*

the adjective has comparative and superlative forms.

the adverb has comparative and superlative forms.

How to keep a reading journal

A reading journal is partly a diary (it records the writer's thoughts, emotions, etc.) and partly a class notebook (it examines a literary text). It allows you to:
- preserve and examine early thoughts and emotions;
- generate ideas and unexpected insights;
- keep track of the way your thoughts and emotions change during the reading process.

Here are some points you may want to consider when writing your journal:

1. **plot development**.
- Speculate about the significance of the title.
- How do you feel after reading the first chapter(s)?
- Which expectations are fulfilled, or not? Why not?
- Which parts were important/funny/exciting/shocking/heart-warming/(un)believable/boring/surprising/confusing?
- Do you like the ending? Does the title (still) fit?

2. the **characters** and the world they live in.
- Do any of the characters remind you of yourself or people you know? Write down any memories that come to mind as you read. Compare your behaviour with that of the characters.
- Would you like to be friends with any of the characters? Is there anybody you dislike? Why?
- What connections are there between the fictional world of this book and your own world?

3. the **message** and the **target group**.
- What do you think the author is saying about life?
- What questions would you like an answer to?
- Has the book changed how you think or helped you?
- Who do you think should read the book?

4. **linguistic** and **artistic features**.
- Study the point of view in a novel or short story. Do you find it suitable for the plot and the message?
- Note the key words and images. How are they connected with the main themes, the structure, etc.?
- Why does the author begin or end a chapter or scene at a certain point? How are units connected?
- Are there any gaps that the author expects you to fill?
- Are the characters and plot believable?

Procedure for writing your journal

1. Use an extra notebook.
2. Reading journals are not formal essays. You may use phrases, sentence fragments, lists, etc.
3. Before you start, you might write down previous experiences with literary texts, things you already know about the book and your expectations of it.
4. Make double entries: Write excerpts from the text on the left and your responses on the right. E.g.
   - definitions of words you would like to explain;
   - words or phrases that seem important;
   - questions about difficult/interesting passages, plus attempts to answer them;
   - comparisons with other reading experiences/texts;
   - images that come to mind while reading a passage;
   - helpful reading strategies;
   - feelings, impressions, etc. triggered by the text;
   - predictions you want to make.
5. Make your entry once you have finished a chapter. Then, reread previous entries. You could compare your expectations with new insights and make predictions about new developments.
6. When you have finished the text look for patterns and identify issues you would like to discuss in class.
7. Rewrite your reading journal if you want to:
   - present your studies in class;
   - write an interpretation for homework or a class test;
   - do follow-up activities.
8. If you exchange journals with one or more partners, you could compare and discuss your findings, or summarise the entries made by three to six students about a particular scene or chapter.

How to create a geographical map

A story map is the visual record of the plot of a short story or novel. You can work on it as you read.

Stage 1: While you read, keep a record of important events. When and where do they happen? How are the different locations related?

Stage 2: If necessary, rearrange events chronologically.

Stage 3: Draw a story map which includes all of the locations where parts of the story are set.

Stage 4: Prepare a short talk in which you:
- explain the details on your map;
- say what happens in the different locations;
- explain who is involved in the events;
- possibly define the point of view used in the story and describe the atmosphere and its effect on the reader.

How to draw a mood chart

A mood chart follows the development of a plot in a short story, novel or play and also records the effects of plot changes on one or more of the characters.
Step 1: Draw a horizontal line starting at zero to mark the beginning of the story. Then draw a vertical line through zero with a scale from +10 (positive feelings) to –10 (negative feelings).
Step 2: As you read through the text, mark important events on the chart according to the character's state of mind at the time. Work from left to right.
Step 3: Join up the marks to show the ups and downs experienced by the character.
Step 4: Collect adjectives which you can use to describe the character's moods, e.g. aggressive, angry, anxious, calm, carefree... You can use the words and the curve to explain a character's development, actions, etc.

Listening

It is impossible to have a conversation with someone if you do not understand what they are saying. In other words, listening is a very important skill. Very often, however, you do not need to understand every single word but only the gist, that is, the general meaning or the most important points. Listen actively to English news, music, etc. as often as possible. This will help you to get used to different accents, and you might also come across interesting phrases/idioms/expressions which you can add to your active vocabulary.
There are different ways of approaching listening tasks. A few suggestions are given below:

– If you need or want to understand a spoken text in more detail, you should concentrate on listening for **key words**, i.e. terms that are often used in a sense unit of the text. Sometimes you may have to find a key word of your own to sum up what is being said.
– **Taking notes** also helps when you listen to a spoken text, as this will remind you of the main points afterwards.
– If you know in advance what a longer listening text is going to be about, you could make up a suitable **grid** so that you can take notes in a systematic way. E.g.

	view of school	view of life
Terry's ...		
His father's ...		

– If you are only interested in whether special points are mentioned or not, you could work with a **checklist**. Before you listen you should make a list of points which you think might be mentioned, including things you would like to know. When you listen to the text you can simply tick off the items, cross out others and add new ones which are brought up.
– If you would like to understand a spoken text word for word, and if you can listen to it several times, you could try to write a **transcript** of the spoken text. This is a fairly difficult task and certainly easier and more fun as a group activity. Think about the context so that you can guess the meaning of words, and make use of dictionaries. If you do this with a pop song, try to get hold of a copy of the text and compare your transcript with the original.
– If you do not know a particular word or expression and you feel it is very important, you should listen to the passage a few times. You can also often solve the problem if you work with a partner or in a team. (Don't forget if you have to look up a word in a dictionary, you may have to try different spelling variations!)

How to take notes

Taking notes means writing down information from a spoken source (speech, interview, etc.) in short form. Here are some tips on how to take notes effectively:

1. Only write down the most important information. It is impossible to note down everything.
2. Only write down key words (nouns, adjectives, verbs, etc.) or key phrases, but never complete sentences.
3. Try to order your notes systematically. If possible, use headings, sub-headings or grids.
4. Use symbols for certain relationships, for example: = ≠ –>
5. Make sure that you can read your handwriting!

Working with audio-visual materials

I Camera operations

Basic vocabulary: shot *(Aufnahme)* uninterrupted sequence of pictures; cut *(Schnitt)* switch from one shot to the next.
Cf. pages 113–114 for more help when talking about camera operations.

Field size
(Bildausschnitt/Bildgröße)

long shot *(Totale)* people/objects shown from a distance

full shot: shot of the whole body/object

medium shot: upper body/part of an object

closeup *(Nahaufnahme)*: head and shoulders

extreme closeup:- *(Detailaufnahme)* face only; detailed shot

Camera movements

static shot: camera does not move

to pan left/right *horizontal schwenken;* to tilt up/down *vertikal schwenken*

crane shot (*Kranfahrt*): camera moves flexibly in all directions on a crane

to zoom in on/out of s.th. (e.g. a face)

tracking shot *(Kamerafahrt)*: camera is on a vehicle moving on the ground

Camera positions

E.g. A point-of-view shot is seen through a character's eyes. Other examples are:

establishing shot: shows location (long shot/pan) at the start of a scene

overhead shot: bird's eye view

over-the-shoulder shot

reverse-angle shot: from the opposite side, usu. shows a dialogue partner

Camera angles

high-angle shot (from above)

eye-level shot

low-angle shot (from below)

II How to analyse a film scene

When analysing a film scene, you could consider the following points.

Narrative elements: Many of the terms used to talk about narrative texts can be applied to films, too (cf. glossary of literary terms, p. 124 or *short story* p. 27):
characters: major/minor characters, round/flat characters, protagonist/antagonist
plot: setting, atmosphere; exposition, immediate beginning (*in medias res*); conflict, crisis, turning-point, climax, action, dialogue, suspense; surprise/happy/unhappy/open ending

Cinematic point of view In a film, point of view depends on camera placement and unlike a literary point of view, it is rarely consistent and often changes from one shot to the next. There are basically two cinematic points of view:

- an *objective point of view*. The camera is like a window through which the viewer observes people and events. This point of view mostly uses a static camera and straightforward camera positioning and angles to ensure that we see the action from the viewpoint of an impersonal observer.
- a *subjective point of view*. The camera shows the action directly from a film character's viewpoint, i.e. as seen through his/her eyes or over his/her shoulder. Alternatively, an indirect-subjective point of view brings us close to the action so that we feel involved, e.g. through a closeup of a face or an unusual camera position or angle.

• Use freeze frames to illustrate how the point of view changes or remains consistent. How does this influence the way the viewer sees the scene?

• Is one point of view predominant in the scene? What effect does this have?

Audience empathy is a viewer's ability to understand a film character's feelings as if they were his/her own. A filmmaker usually gets the audience to love the protagonist and hate the antagonist. Empathy towards the protagonist should be created as early as possible. This is done by showing him/her in crises where he/she suffers from danger, loneliness, unkindness, insecurity, humiliation, etc.

In general, characters in popular films are larger than life, yet still emotionally accessible to the audience. A viewer who recognizes his/her own struggles and ambitions on screen will follow the story with interest.

• Does the scene create a certain mood or emotional response, e.g. does it scare you, make you feel romantic, make you laugh...? What techniques are used to achieve this? Cf. the sections on cinematic point of viewand special effects for ideas.

WB: pages 52–56

• Does the scene change your feelings towards the protagonist or the other characters in any way? Why, or why not?

• Is the viewer directly informed about a character's thoughts, e.g. through voice-over narration? Are there any indirect hints at a character's thoughts/emotions, e.g. in body language or tone of voice?

Special effects

• Are special effects used in the scene? If so, describe them and explain their effect. Consider these points.

Computer-generated imaging: It is possible to create realistic three-dimensional images using computer programmes. These images are integrated into films to turn artificial figures into convincing characters, to improve images and to create locations.

Slow motion: The action is shown at a slower speed than normal to intensify the moment, to exaggerate effort or frustration, to suggest superhuman speed/power and so on.

Flashback: A scene shows past events, e.g. to provide background information, to recall s.th. in the past, to break up the chronological narration

Visual symbols: An object stands for s.th. else, e.g. a setting can have symbolic overtones; a symbol may be universally understood, e.g. the American flag, the cross, or only take on a meaning in the context of the film, e.g. through repetition or special visual emphasis.

Voice-over narration: A voice speaking offscreen gives background information, fills in gaps in the story, or reveals a character's thoughts. If it is extensively used for a character, it conveys the impression of a first-person narrator.

Film music: It may show a mood or a character's emotions, evoke nostalgic feelings for a past era, foreshadow an event (e.g. a murder), build suspense, provide transitions between scenes, etc.

Hand-held camera: The uneven movement heightens the impression of reality, e.g. in filming violent scenes.

Camera operations

• Divide the length of the scene by the number of shots. Comment on the average length of a shot, e.g. a number of short shots create the impression of fast-paced action, a sequence of long shots may focus the viewer's attention on the emotional significance of a situation.

• Describe the use of the camera in the scene. What is the advantage/effect/function of unusual camera operations? Consider the following:
characters: characterizes people indirectly; shows a character's emotions; draws attention to certain people or objects
plot: describes the setting; evokes a certain atmosphere; changes the speed of the action; creates suspense
audience empathy: shows the action from s.o.'s point of view/through s.o.'s eyes; influences the extent to which we identify with a character

III How to prepare the filming of a scene

1st option: storyboard
In real life, a film director usually works with one or more illustrators who visualize key shots from the screenplay in a sequence of drawings. These sketches give the film crew a first impression of what the director's ideas are for the filming of a scene. A board with these pictures is the basis for the actual shooting.
• Develop a storyboard in groups. At least one student should be good at drawing. Use a separate sheet for each key shot. Include a rough sketch of the image, and basic information about the shot. Display your sequence of shots in class by glueing your sheets onto a poster. A storyboard could look like the one on the right.

shot no. ________

setting/characters/action

dialogue

camera angle/movement

sound effects/music

2nd option: shooting script (as a grid)
Alternatively, a grid like the one below can be used to show ideas for the shooting of a scene:

shot no.	setting/ characters/ action	dialogue	camera angle/ movement	sound/ music

How to analyse a documentary, news report

WB: page 51

A documentary is a film or video which examines a topic in a factual way. It may include interviews, archive material, statistics and, of course, various viewpoints. They may be balanced by including different opinions or may be subjective and only present the viewpoint of one producer.
When you analyse a documentary, you could look at the following points:
- the *topic and its aspects*: What is the main topic? Which aspects are dealt with? (What sense units do you find, and what does each one deal with?)
- *visual material*: Do the pictures speak for themselves? Is the visual material staged, or was it filmed live? Is any visual background material used, e.g. statistics, charts, archive material?
- *spoken material*: Do we hear any dialogues between the people involved? If there are interviews included, what are they about? Are the pictures commented on by a speaker (voice-over)? Does he/she use formal language, or is his/her style conversational?
- *link between the voice-over and the picture:* What is the function of the voice-over? Does it describe what we see and/or give other information? Would we understand as much without the pictures?
- *balance or bias:* Is the topic presented from different angles? Is a full range of opinions presented? What other background material, e.g. statistics is given? Is there a variety of opinions from experts and/or eye-witnesses?
  Does the voice-over express a particular attitude or evaluate what is shown? Is his/her voice neutral or emotional?
- *conclusions:* What conclusions are drawn at the end?

How to understand advertisements

A lot of advertisements want to sell something or get people to support a particular group or organization – you are one of the potential buyers or supporters. Advertisers often want you to follow them blindly, so do not let yourself be fooled! Here are some helpful tips for things to consider when you are looking at ads:

- Study the layout – what catches your attention first? How is your eye drawn to the product/brand name? Are there visual elements aimed at influencing you subconsciously?
- Study the photos, drawings, etc. – do they represent the world you know, or do they present an ideal?
- Does the advertisement quote findings, e.g. statistics? If yes, do they give the whole truth, or do they leave out important aspects?
- Study the text type (see page 55) – does the text aim to convince, persuade or manipulate you? What techniques are used to do so? How does the text expand on the tag line, slogan or photo/drawing?
- Does the advertisement use rhetorical devices (see page 121)? If yes, what is their effect?
- Study the train of thoughts – are all the elements arranged and connected logically?

How to work with commercials

WB: page 50

If possible, try to get hold of a commercial in English. Here are some ideas as to how you can work with it:

- Discuss what makes it worthwhile analysing. Does it show people in a real or ideal world? Does it have an interesting storyline, or a catchy tag line or jingle?
- What kinds of camera angles are used and how effective are they? (See page 112 for help.)
- What role does the product play in the commercial?

Class presentation: You could either cover the screen and let the class listen to the programme, or show the pictures without the sound first. Alternatively, you could work with freeze frames or stop the video at a certain point to get a discussion going. Discuss your ideas with your teacher if you feel you want help.

How to analyse a music video

WB: page 49

Consider these ideas when you analyse music videos.

- What images or ideals are presented? What kind of world is shown, a real world, an imaginary one, a nightmare?
- What mood does the film/music create, and how?
- Does the material tell a story or evoke associations and feelings?
- What are the most interesting elements? E.g. music, pictures, lyrics…
- What message, if any, do the lyrics have?
- What makes the visual elements interesting? E.g. unusual pictures and/or camera angles, the speed of the film, unusual cuts, special effects…
- What particular elements do you notice in the video? See the table below for ideas.

<table>
<tr><th rowspan="2">PERFORMANCE CLIP</th><th rowspan="2">CONCEPT PERFORMANCE</th><th colspan="2">CONCEPT CLIP</th></tr>
<tr><th>narrative</th><th>associative/abstract</th></tr>
<tr><td>singer/band as performers</td><td>singer/band as actors</td><td colspan="2">singer/band do not act themselves</td></tr>
<tr><td rowspan="2">performance documentary
– presents a live concert;
– interaction between singer/band and audience

enhanced performance
– studio performance plus outdoor locations,
– usually a song and dance number</td><td rowspan="2">– film action often illustrates lyrics;
– performance sometimes includes associative visual elements (see concept clips)</td><td>– illustration of lyrics
– chronological context of actions, or a sequence of short shots (montage)</td><td>– no plot
– pictures often based on the mood of the lyrics
– pictures often independent of the music</td></tr>
<tr><td colspan="2">– excessive montage
– frequent cuts
– frequent change of camera position
– extreme camera angles
– many special effects/much digital processing</td></tr>
</table>

Writing

How to quote

A quotation is a phrase or sentence taken from another piece of writing. Quotations are often used to prove a point or support an argument. Quotation marks ("...") are used to show where the quotation begins and ends.

E.g. In lines 8–12, the text says "..."

Note: Any change in the quotation must be put into brackets like these: [...].

How to write a summary

WB: pages 36–37

I The summary of a **non-fictional text** presents the most important points of this text. The following suggestions might help you:

1. Concentrate on the basic ideas, facts and arguments.
2. Leave out details, examples, quotations, dialogue and, most important of all, your personal opinion.
3. Read the text several times. After reading the text once to find out what it is about, make notes on the most important points.
4. Making a **key word outline** can be useful. Sometimes key words – expressions or topics a paragraph may deal with – are used in the text. Sometimes you may have to find one to sum up the contents of the paragraph.
5. Use these notes as the basis of your summary. Think about how you could express the main ideas from the text differently (using synonyms, paraphrasing, etc.).
6. Your summary should be between one third and one fifth of the original text.

II When you are asked to write a summary of a **fictional text,** this usually refers to the plot of a short story, novel or play. (The plot says what happens, and why.)

Here are some tips for writing a plot summary:

1. Briefly describe the setting and the characters, then say what happens and how the events are logically connected.
2. Base your summary on the text: this is not the place for interpretation and analysis.
3. Avoid direct speech.
4. Use the present tense.
5. As far as possible, use your own words.

How to write an essay (short/extensive)

WB: pages 30–32

Both in a *Klausur* and in an international language exam, you are expected to write a short essay in a limited time period. Here are some ideas to help you:

There is no such thing as 'the' essay. The two most common types, however, are the expository essay, in which you present a situation or explain an idea, and the argumentative essay, in which you discuss a controversial topic. All essays, however, should be well-planned and clearly structured.

Planning

– Take five minutes to write down relevant ideas. Do not collect too many as this will confuse you.

– Decide on the position you want to take.

– Put your ideas into a logical order, e.g. number them.

Writing

– Begin with a thesis statement, i.e. a sentence/short paragraph that presents the main idea of the essay and helps you to focus on one central point.

– In an expository essay, present two or three stages of a development or aspects of a problem. Use examples to explain what you mean. Write a conclusion in which you summarize your findings or outline possible consequences.

– In an argumentative (or persuasive) essay state why the problem is controversial. Present a few views that are opposed to/different from your own position (cons). Define your position or put forward one or two arguments that support it (pros). Use examples and write a logical conclusion based on your arguments. Try not to use the most obvious examples that everybody else will come up with as well.

An extensive essay, which you may have to write for homework, takes longer to write. You should stick to the rules that apply to the short essay as well as:

- dealing with the topic in a more complex way.
- collecting more ideas and refer to a larger number of aspects or mention more details.
- taking more time to develop the line of argument and structure the essay.

How to write a dramatic text

A dramatic text usually consists of three parts: the introduction, the dialogue and the stage directions. As a guideline, you could try the following approach:

1. Start with a general introduction including:
   a) the setting: (time of action: year, season,… and place of action: country, city,…);
   b) the characters: (name, age);
   c) a brief outline of the situation at the beginning: e.g. the stage, position/appearance of the characters.
2. Write the dialogue.
   Susan:…
   Fred:…
   Susan:…
3. Add stage directions where necessary to inform the reader/actor/actress how the characters should move and speak. Adverbs are very popular!
   Susan *(excitedly)*:…
   Fred *(is silent for a moment, then shouts angrily)*:…

How to write a radio play

A radio play is a dramatic text for the radio. When writing a radio play, you have to keep in mind that this kind of play is for listening only. Here are some tips on how to cope with this limitation:

1. Begin by deciding on the characters (name, age, relationship between them, job) and whether you want a narrator or not.
2. It might be a good idea to start the action with one character speaking to the listeners. As a kind of first-person narrator, he/she could introduce the setting, the characters and the situation at the beginning: *I am not really a shy person but when I saw…* This narrator could then also make comments between the scenes, e.g. about what has happened in the meantime, preparing the listeners for the next scene, voicing his/her own opinion, etc.
3. Decide on a sequence of scenes. You may introduce a scene with a few words by the narrator, or you might also suggest noises typical of the setting, e.g. *the door bell rings,* and then let the dialogue speak for itself.
4. Don't forget that all the directions must refer to noises or sounds (e.g. *laughter, music, bells ringing, etc.)* or the tone in which something is said (e.g. *angrily, excitedly, etc.)* but not the movements of the speakers or the description of the furniture.
5. You might want to show the beginning and end of a scene by fading in and fading out the voices.

How to write a sketch

A sketch is a special type of drama. If you are asked to write a sketch, it should be:

1. short and self-contained (there should be a clear beginning and ending);
2. humorous, possibly with a punchline at the end;
3. based on the quick exchange of remarks;
4. limited in the number of characters (2–3).

How to write short stories

WB: pages 34–35

I If you want to write a classical **'plot story'** with the emphasis on action and suspense:

1. Choose an interesting scene/meeting/experience with two or three characters.
2. The action should start in the very first sentence.
3. After the beginning, describe the setting to create a certain atmosphere.
4. Develop the action step by step up to a climax at the end, or include a turning-point in the middle which takes your story in an unexpected direction.
5. Conclude with a surprise or open ending.

You could write your short story in pairs/groups.

II If you want to write a **'slice-of-life story'** with the emphasis on character and psychology:

1. Choose a main character and an important moment in his/her life.
2. Describe the setting in detail to create a certain atmosphere.
3. Show the different reactions/opinions/motives of the other characters.
4. Focus on thoughts and feelings, not on plot and suspense.
5. Finish with an open ending.

You could write your short story in pairs/groups.

How to write a poem

WB: page 38

The following ideas will show you some different ways of writing a poem:

1. Read through the poems in the book on pages 10, 74, 75 and 98 to gather ideas.
2. Write down the associations you have with the subject and then add verbs to form phrases.
3. Find a central image or symbol around which you could write your poem.
4. Use each letter of the subject word/phrase (e.g. love) as the beginning of the first word in each line.
5. Remember, your poem does not have to rhyme or have a regular rhythm. Choose a form that you feel happy with.

Note: You might even decide to write your poem in groups – each person could contribute one line.

How to write a letter

WB: pages 40–41

There are basically two types of letter – the personal letter and the formal letter. In an informal letter, e.g. to a friend, you are free to choose your own form and language. In a formal letter, e.g. applying for a job, you have to follow certain rules:

1. Address and date:
- Write your own address, without your name, in the top right-hand corner and the date below this. It is not usual to write the place name before the date.
- Write the receiver's name and address on the left-hand side but lower than your address.

2. Beginning and ending:
- In formal letters you should begin and end as follows: *Dear Sir/Madam … Yours faithfully* + your name, or *Dear Mr/Mrs/Ms … Yours sincerely* + your name.
- You should begin the first paragraph with a capital letter.
- At the end of the text, use a closing phrase like *I'm looking forward to hearing from you soon* or *Thank you very much in advance for your help.*

Note: Only personal letters have endings like *Love, All the best, See you soon.*

How to write a letter to the editor

WB: page 42

A letter to the editor of a newspaper is a formal letter in which the reader can express his/her support for or criticism of an article, event or opinion previously published in the newspaper.

- Your letter should be short and to the point.
- You could briefly state which article/statements you are referring to at the beginning of your letter and then express your opinion clearly but politely.

How to write a curriculum vitae (CV)

- Your CV should be well-structured and arranged clearly.
- Make sure the information fits on one page.
- Always give the dates when you did something, e.g. when you attended what school, when you did a summer job, etc. You should then arrange these points with the most recent listed first.
- Think which of your interests are most relevant for the job application and put these first. Only include interests or hobbies which are genuine: don't put in extra ones just to fill up the space.
- Give the names and addresses of two referees, i.e. people who will be prepared to write you a reference. Choose people who know you well, e.g. a teacher, someone you have worked for, etc. But don't forget to ask them before you include them!

```
Curriculum Vitae

Name:…
Address:…
Date and place of birth:…
Current age:…

Schools attended:
-…

Examination results:
- …

Work experience:
- …

Interests:
- …

Referees' names and addresses:
- …
```

Communicating

I Expressing opinions

WB: pp. 45, 47

Giving an opinion

In my opinion/view...
To my mind...
I am sure/convinced that...
I think/believe/feel that...
I am of the opinion that...
It seems to me that...

Asking for someone's opinion

What do you think about...?
How do you feel about...?
What's your opinion on/about...?
Would you like to comment on...?

Agreeing and disagreeing

↑
You are quite/absolutely right.
I (completely) agree with you.
Exactly.
I think you are right.
You're right up to a point.
You might/could be right.
I wouldn't quite say that.
Do you really think so?
I don't think that's right.
You can't really say that.
That's not true at all.
I disagree entirely.
↓

II Acting and reacting

Interrupting

May I interrupt you?
Did I understand you correctly?
Sorry, would you mind explaining...?
I'm afraid I can't follow. Would you mind explaining...?
Excuse me, could you repeat/explain that again?

Clarifying

Yes, that's exactly what I mean.
The point I'm trying to make is (that)...

Defending

That's not what I was trying to say.
That's not what I meant. I was trying to...
You've misunderstood me completely.

Making suggestions

How about...?
It might be a good idea to...
I would suggest/recommend that...
We should/could...
If I were you, I would...

Playing for time

Actually/As a matter of fact/To be quite honest...
What I'm trying to say is that...
Just let me get this right...
How shall I put/say this ?
I must admit, that's a good question.

III Presenting an argument

WB: p. 47

Beginning

I would like to say something about...
I would like to comment on (the problem of)...
There are three points I would like to make.

Ordering

First of all/To start with...
Firstly,... Secondly,... Finally,...
At first..., but then...

Adding

In addition,...
I'd like to add that...
Another point is that...

Balancing

On the one hand..., but on the other (hand)...
Although..., we mustn't forget that...
Whereas..., we have to remember that...
In contrast to... However...

Drawing conclusions

That's why.../For this reason...
Therefore/As a result/Consequently...

Summarizing

To sum up,...
In short/All in all,...
I'd like to finish by saying this...

Learning vocabulary

WB: pages 18–29

Now that you are a more advanced learner of English, you should start taking over responsibility for learning vocabulary. The more words and structures you have, the better you will be able to communicate. Many of the books you will be working with (and the English texts you come across outside school, e.g. pop songs, articles in magazines, etc.) do not contain a vocabulary list or tell you which words you should learn. So, whenever you read a text, you should note down any English words and phrases you find interesting and useful. Some students write down everything in a vocabulary book, others prefer to use a box of file-cards or a computer file, where they can arrange the words and structures as they see fit. Here are some tips on how to do this more effectively:

a) **Alphabetical order, dictionary-style** is useful if you remember the word but not its exact meaning or spelling, etc. But it is useless if you have an idea but do not have the words to express it.

b) **Word families** contain all the words derived from one particular word, often by adding prefixes or suffixes (see below), e.g. *appear/disappear/appearance,* etc.

c) **Synonyms and antonyms** i.e. words of identical meaning (e.g. *clever, intelligent, smart,* etc.) and opposites *(clever – stupid).* This works like dominoes – if you remember one, you can (hopefully) remember the others.

d) **Semantic fields** i.e. grouping words of related meanings. See the box on page 89.

e) **Collocations** i.e. words which frequently appear connected with each other (e.g. *to make friends; to fall in love,* etc.). If you find them as a unit, note them down as a unit. You will most likely remember them as a unit when you need them.

f) **Mind maps** (see page 63) or **topic webs**. These methods are similar to the semantic fields, as you are collecting vocabulary on a particular topic. However, they do it on a larger scale. Topic webs are objective and are more structured than mind maps.

Here is the beginning of a topic web on newspapers:

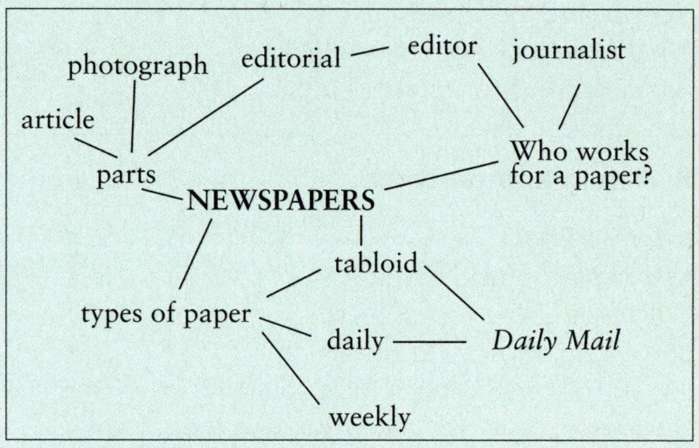

But above all remember: There is not *one* particular method for learning and remembering words. You should try and find the one(s) best suited to you.

Recognizing common prefixes …

	meaning	example
in-	not/opposite of	**in**dependence
im- + *b, m, p*		**im**possible
il- + *il;* **ir-** + *r*		**il**logical; **ir**rational
un-	not/opposite of/ reverse of	**un**important
dis-		**dis**appear
de-	reverse/take away	**de**value
mis-	wrong	**mis**understand
re-	again/back	**re**write
over-	too much	**over**emphasize
under-	too little	**under**pay
super-	over/more than	**super**human
sub-	under/less than	**sub**standard
inter-	between/among	**inter**national
trans-	across	**trans**atlantic
co-	together	**co**-operation
pre-	before	**pre**historic
post-	after	**post**war

… and suffixes

adjective	**->**	**noun** (quality/state)
close	**-ness**	closeness
certain	**-(i)ty**	certainty
different	**-ence**	difference
true	**-th**	truth
verb	**->**	**noun** (activity/process)
to develop	**-ment**	development
to create	**-ion**	creation
to realize	**-ation**	realization
to decide	**-ision**	decision
verb	**->**	**noun** (tool/s.o. who does s.th.)
to mix; to act	**-er**; **-or**	mixer; actor
verb	**->**	**noun** (process/result)
to begin	**-ing**	beginning

Focus on register and style

Register

Register is a linguistic term and refers to the type of language used by a particular speaker/writer in a particular situation. Registers which are often used are formal language, colloquial language or slang. The register used depends on:

- the *situation*. A speech made at a formal meeting will have a different register than a speech made at a wedding. The same is true of an article in a teenage magazine and an article in a quality newspaper.
- the *audience*. A scientist will speak differently to a group of non-specialists about his/her field of expertise than he/she would in a presentation to a group of scientists. The same scientist will use a different register again with his/her children.
- the *topic*. Many fields such as science, journalism (journalese) and advertising have a special register.

Analysing register

When you are examining register, you should look at:

- the *type of language*. Is it formal or informal such as colloquial language (conversational) or slang? Formal language suggests a distance between speaker/listener and writer/reader, while informal language implies closeness.
- the *vocabulary*. Are technical words used from areas such as science, technology, medicine, etc.?
- the *syntax*: Are sentences generally short and easy to understand or long and complicated? Is the language informal with few structures (restricted code) or is it formal and educated with a wide range of structures (elaborated code)? Is there a mixture of short and long sentences? Is there a preference for main clauses or are there a lot of different subclauses implying more complex structures?

When analysing register, you could proceed as follows:

1. Mark the linguistic features you find in the text with different-coloured markers.
2. Gather your findings in a grid. You could use the headings *type of language, vocabulary* and *syntax*. Note suitable examples from the text/speech, etc.
3. Decide which of the examples you want to use in your analysis of register. Then, rearrange the columns in the order in which you will mention them.
4. Remember your findings are only pieces in a puzzle which must be combined to get a full picture of the register. In particular, you must consider what particular effect the speaker/writer wants to create by using a particular linguistic feature when talking to a particular listener about a particular topic.

Rhetorical devices

Rhetorical devices in spoken or written language are used as a means of persuasion. Examples of rhetorical devices include: alliteration, assonance, hyperbole, irony, sarcasm and understatement (see pages 124–125 for more information about these terms).

Using rhetorical devices in talks

In a talk the speaker often:

- repeats *key words,* e.g. to stress/emphasize an idea;
- uses *quotations* or *proverbs,* e.g. to support a statement;
- asks *rhetorical questions,* e.g. to structure the talk/to get the listeners thinking/to involve the audience;
- uses *personal pronouns* like "we/our/you", e.g. to address the audience personally/to establish contact;
- makes an *appeal* to the audience, e.g. to make his/her aims clear/to win the listeners' support/to end the talk effectively.

Imagery (figures of speech)

Images express a thought indirectly, that is figuratively rather than literally. Examples of imagery are metaphors, similes, personification and symbols (see pages 124–125 for more information about these terms).

Looking at the function of imagery

An author may use images:

- to describe s.th. visually/more vividly;
- to explain s.th. graphically;
- to express s.th. so that it is easily remembered;
- to arouse certain associations;
- to evoke particular emotions and responses;
- to be humorous.

Projects

Gathering information

For some projects you have to find further information. Here are some ideas where to look or who to ask:

- other pupils and teachers/family/friends
- school or local library:
  - books, e.g. encyclopedias/specialist books
  - newspapers/magazines
  - address books in the reference section of a larger library
- information agencies, e.g. USIS (United States Information Service)
- government agencies, e.g. the British Council
- informative computer programmes, e.g. Encarta
- Internet

Note: Don't forget to write the source down carefully, in case you want to quote from the book, or refer to it again. You should write down the title, the author, the publisher, the place and date of publication as well as the page and/or line numbers.

Conducting a survey

WB: page 43

If you want to find out what other people think, do, etc., you can conduct a survey in order to get objective information. A survey is often carried out using a questionnaire, i.e. a list of questions. When making up a questionnaire, you should think about the following:

1. Allow people enough time to answer the questions.
2. Ask clear questions and list them systematically.
3. You may ask questions
   a) which ask for a free answer;
   b) with a choice of answers and boxes to be ticked;
   c) which can be answered on a five-point scale.
   Don't forget to leave enough space for the answers!
4. Remember that it is often useful if you can present your findings in the form of statistics or diagrams.

Producing a newspaper

WB: page 33

Step 1: At your first staff meeting, you should decide on what topics you want to deal with and what information you have to gather. You should appoint members of staff to gather information (see above), do interviews (see page 107), conduct surveys (see above), take photos, etc.
Step 2: Carry out the tasks assigned to you.
Step 3: At the next staff meeting, analyse the material and decide on what types of article are to be written (i.e. argumentative, persuasive, etc. – see box on page 55), and by whom.
Step 4: Write the articles.
Step 5: At a third staff meeting, you should edit the articles, and decide on the headlines – remember they must be eye-catchers!
Step 6: At the next meeting, you should think about the layout. Decide on which article to put first, what photos to put where, how big you want the headlines, etc. (You may have to shorten articles.)
Step 7: The paper can now be printed or reproduced (the computer enthusiasts in your group can have fun now!). You could even send a copy to your partner school.

Producing a radio programme

Before you begin, decide on how many contributors you are going to have.
Step 1: Plan the structure of the programme carefully, always keeping your potential listeners in mind.
Step 2: Arrange spoken contributions in a logical order, but make sure the audience expects something even more interesting from the next contribution.
Step 3: To capture the attention of the audience, start your programme with a popular song (or part of it), then introduce your topic with a provocative or humorous statement, or with a short introduction of yourself.
Step 4: Keep the individual spoken contributions short (a lot can be said in two minutes!), and make sure you end with an open question or by introducing the topic of your next contribution.
Step 5: Find suitable music to link the spoken contributions. Ideally it should be connected with the theme.

Note: Don't forget, the presentation is very important. The presenters lead the audience through the programme. They introduce new topics and link the individual contributions.

Acting out a dramatic text

Step 0: Read the text several times, checking the pronunciation of new words using a dictionary. A thorough understanding of the action and the characters is essential when you are staging a dramatic text.
Step 1: Form a group. The size depends on the number of characters in the text, plus one (the director).
Step 2: Distribute the roles. You should agree on who takes over the role of director. The person chosen should be generally accepted as being the 'boss'. He/she:
- is responsible for the success of the performance;
- should think about the movements of the actors/actresses as well as which props are needed. (Don't forget to refer to the stage directions!);
- advises the actors on their acting and intonation.

Step 3: Depending on the time available, you may decide to shorten the text or to concentrate on only one part. Keep in mind that the actors/actresses should learn their parts by heart.
Step 4: Sit down in a circle. Read the text several times, focusing on the correct pronunciation and intonation.
Step 5: The performance should now be rehearsed on stage. Think about movements and gestures – the actors/actresses may still refer to the text, if they need to.
Step 6: In the final phase, the actors/actresses should recite their parts from memory and no longer refer to the text. The director should give them help if necessary.
Step 7: Act out the play in front of an audience.
To involve the audience, the director could give explanations and comments at a press conference afterwards, answering questions from the other students (i.e. reporters).

Remember: Everyone should consider the project a fun activity. The process is more important than the product!

Turning a prose text into a film scene

Step 1: Get into groups. The size depends on the number of characters in your text plus two (the director and the camera operator).
Step 2: Using different colours, highlight the following information in your text:
- time and place of action (setting);
- the characters: age, job, outward appearance;
- actions/movements;
- feelings/thoughts;
- direct/indirect speech;
- comments of the (third-person) narrator.

Think about how you can present this information effectively in a screenplay.
Step 3: Turn the text into a screenplay. You might want to start by introducing:
- the characters: name, age, job;
- the setting: time (year, season,...) and place of action (country, city,...);
- the situation at the beginning, e.g. the outward appearance of the characters.

Think of how this can be presented, i.e. through dialogue, actions, etc. Then write the dialogue. Include directions for the actors/actresses where necessary. Try to keep as close as possible to the original text. If you change the dialogue, give reasons for your decision.
Step 4: Add instructions to the script for the camera operator.
Step 5: Rehearse the scene first with the text, then without the text. When you are satisfied with the performance, film it.

Marketing a film idea

In order to convince a film company of your film idea, you have to prepare an attractive 'information pack'.
Step 1: Sum up the action in a few sentences.
Step 2: Give reasons why the theme could be commercially successful.
Step 3: Suggest a catchy title.
Step 4: Outline a possible sequence of scenes (characters, setting, conflict, topic of dialogue).
Step 5: Describe the characters.
Step 6: Suggest actors ('the ideal cast') and the type of music.
Step 7: Write a text advertising the film.
Step 8: Design a film poster.
Step 9: Now try to convince the director of the film company of your ideas!
Although most of the tasks should be done as a group activity, certain tasks like steps 7 and 8 could be taken over by one or two members of the group.

Glossary of literary terms

Terms in *italics* refer to main entries in the glossary. The numbers refer to the page where the term appears in a box.

alliteration [-ˌ--'--] the repetition of consonants at the beginning of words or within words. 121

antagonist [-'---] character in a fictional text or *drama* who is opposed to, or in conflict with, the *protagonist.* 87

assonance ['æsənəns] the repetition of vowels in stressed syllables, used for emphasis. 121

atmosphere the tone or mood of a *novel, short story* or *play* created by *setting,* description and *characters.* 27

characters see ***characterization.***

characterization [ˌ----'--] characters in a narrative text can be presented in two ways. The *narrator* or a figure in the text tells the reader what a person is like (direct characterization). Alternatively, the reader has to find out what a person is like through what this character does, says, thinks or feels (indirect characterization). A flat character can be described clearly in a few words. His/her behaviour is predictable, as he/she does not change. A round character is a life-like, complex individual. He/she may be shown in different moods and may change in the course of the action.

connotation associations and emotions a word may evoke. 76

couplet ['kʌplɪt] a *stanza* of two lines.

denotation *literal* meaning of a word. 76

drama a play or drama may consist of several acts which can be subdivided into scenes. The roles or parts are played by actresses and actors, who make up the cast. The characters talk to each other in dialogues. The director helps the actors to put the stage directions (where to stand, how to move and speak) into practice and decides about the use of props (furniture or other objects on the stage). A public performance is prepared through a number of rehearsals. The people who watch the play are called the audience. The author of a play is called a playwright. In English, the term drama also refers to the art of writing and performing a play. 15

euphemism ['ju:fəmɪzəm] a more gentle expression used instead of the more usual one to express unpleasant, frightening or embarrassing facts, e.g. The old dog was put to sleep (i.e. killed). 73

exposition the first part of a *play* or *story.* It gives the information necessary to understand the conflict and events which follow. 27

figurative using images and pictures that must be 'translated' to be understood. 89

free verse a form of *poetry* which is 'free' of *metre* and does not usually *rhyme.*

hyperbole [haɪ'pɜ:bəlɪ] a statement which is exaggerated for effect. 20, 121

imagery images express a thought indirectly, that is *figuratively* rather than *literally.* See also *simile, metaphor, symbol* and *personification.* 121

irony ['aɪrənɪ] saying one thing but meaning another. 16, 121

literal using words in their everyday meaning. 89

metaphor ['metəfə] a comparison between two objects or ideas, without a word of comparison ("like", "as" or "as if"), e.g. "School is hell". 121

metre the regular pattern of stressed and unstressed syllables. 75

mini-saga a story of exactly 50 words. 21

narrator [nə'reɪtə] the person or voice who tells the story in a *novel* or *short story.* The narrator is not identical with the author. The narrator can be a *character* in the text who tells the reader what he/she experiences, thinks and feels, ("I"). This first-person narrator is always limited in his/her view of the events (limited point of view). A third-person narrator is not a character in the narrative but stands outside it. He/She refers to the characters in the story as "he/she/they". A third-person narrator may be an omniscient [ɒm'nɪsɪənt] narrator who knows everything about characters and events (unlimited point of view); a 'selective' third-person narrator who presents the story through one character's eyes (limited point of view) or an unobtrusive third-person narrator who describes the action but not characters' thoughts, etc. 27, 67

novel a long fictional prose text. It often has a large number of *characters*, different *settings* and a complex *plot.* 82

parody ['pærədɪ] speech, text or music that imitates and exaggerates the style of a well-known text in order to be amusing. 20

personification [ˌ----'--] a kind of *metaphor* in which human characteristics or feelings are given to an object, an animal, an abstract idea or a plant, e.g. the door screamed. 121

poetry a *poem* is usually a fairly short piece of writing, divided into single lines. It often expresses the *speaker's* experiences. Traditional poetry makes use of four very important poetic devices: *metre, stanza, rhyme, rhythm.* Modern poetry often does not have a regular *rhythm* or a *rhyme* scheme. 75

play see ***drama***

plot the plot of a *story, novel* or *play* is the sequence of events as arranged by the author. It says what happens, and why. 26

point of view the position or perspective from which the *narrator* presents the story to the reader. See ***narrator.***

protagonist [-'---] the main character in a *novel, play* or *short story.* 27

quatrain ['kwɒ'treɪn] a *stanza* of four lines.

rhyme similarity of sounds in two or more words. Words rhyme when their accented vowels and all following sounds are identical. This often occurs at the end of lines (end rhyme). The pattern created is called a rhyme scheme. It is represented using small letters (see Herrick: abab cdcd…). 75

rhythm ['rɪðm] the flow of language created by the arrangement of unstressed and stressed syllables. It is mainly based on *metre.* 75

sarcasm *irony* which is cutting and meant to hurt. 16, 121

setting the time and place that characterize a work of literature. 27

short story a short story is a short fictional prose text which is meant to be read in a single sitting. It can be as short as 500 and as long as 15,000 words. A lot of short stories follow different patterns but the following points apply to many of them. There may be one main character *(protagonist)* or a group of equally important characters. There is a single *setting* (i.e. the time and place of the action does not change). However, longer short stories might have more than one setting. The setting also helps to create a certain *atmosphere.* The reader may be led into the story through an *exposition.* In modern stories the action often starts immediately in the first sentence. In some stories the action can develop logically through conflicts or crises and finally reaches a climax or turning-point near or at the end (emphasis on action and suspense). Some stories concentrate on a decisive moment in the life of the main *character* (emphasis on character and psychology). There is often a surprise ending, a happy/unhappy ending or an open ending. 27

simile ['sɪmɪlɪ] a comparison between two objects or ideas, using "like", "as" or "as if", e.g. "School is like hell". 10, 121

sketch a short humorous scene often as part of a theatre or television show. 12

sonnet ['--] a sonnet is a very traditional *poem* consisting of 14 lines. It is usually written in iambic pentameter (i.e. five beats per line, each beat consisting of an unstressed and stressed syllable). A sonnet often deals with subjects that deeply move people, such as love or death. Its most common form in English literature is the English (or Shakespearean) sonnet. It consists of a logical sequence of three *quatrains* and a final *couplet* in which a well-worded, general insight or truth is given as a conclusion. Its rhyme scheme is abab cdcd efef gg.

speaker the speaker is the voice speaking to us in a *poem.* He/she is not necessarily identical with the author, even if "I" is used. 11

stanza ['stænzə] the usually regular number of lines which form a unit in a *poem.* 75

suspense the feeling of expectation or excitement aroused in the reader by a well-constructed *plot* about what is going to happen. 26

symbol ['sɪmbl] something concrete (an object, a place, etc.) which stands for an abstract idea, e.g. a rose is a symbol of love. 11, 121

understatement opp. of *hyperbole;* s.th. that is represented as being less important than it really is. 20, 121

Glossary of audio-visual terms

Terms in *italics* refer to main entries in the glossary. The numbers refer to the page where the term appears in a box.

advertisement, ad, advert [əd'vɜ:tɪsmənt] a notice or film sequence designed to sell a product, e.g. in newspapers and magazines and on television. 56

audience empathy is the viewer's ability to understand a film character's feelings as if they were his/her own. 43

cinematic point of view is determined by the position of the camera. It may be objective (the viewer observes people and events as if through a window created by the camera) or subjective (the camera shows the action from a character's viewpoint, i.e. through his/her eyes or over his/her shoulder). 49

commercial an advertisement on the television or the radio. 56

computer generated imaging the creation of realistic, three-dimensional images for films using special computer programmes. 38

director also called a *filmmaker* turns a *screenplay* into a *shooting script* by changing the screenplay and adding instructions for the actors and camera crew. He/She controls and directs everything on the film set. 37

documentary a film which explores in detail a subject of general interest. It may or may not be a topical subject. 61

editor He/She cuts the film shot by the *director* into the final version. 37

filmmaker see *director* 37

flashback a film scene showing events in the past. It is included in the film present. 50

music video a short film featuring the performance of a song. 62

newscast brief information about topical events. 61

news report detailed information about an event. It includes film material and interviews. 61

producer He/She looks after the business side of making a film. 37

product placement the inclusion of products and company logos in a film or television programme as a form of advertising. 37

scriptwriter He/She writes the *screenplay*. 37

screenplay is a play for the screen. It is often based on a novel, a stageplay or a historical event. 37

shooting script a revised version of the *screenplay* which includes instructions for the actors and camera crew. 37

storyboard key scenes in a film are usually visualized in pencil drawings by the director and illustrators before the scenes are shot. The drawings are placed on a board and are used as the basis for the shooting. 39

voice-over the voice of a narrator speaking offscreen. 50

Index

Terms in *italics* refer to entries in the *strategy pages*. For index of literary terms and of media terms see the glossary on pages 124–126.

Picture credits

The editors wish to thank all authors, publishers and photo agencies who have given permission to use copyright material. Sources are given underneath the texts. The following list acknowledges copyright holders who are not identical with the publishers quoted and also includes additional specifications demanded by copyright holders.
Every effort has been made to trace owners of copyright material, but in a few cases this has not proved possible and repeated enquiries have remained unanswered. The publishers would be glad to hear from any further copyright owners of material reproduced in this book.

© Adrienne Salinger, San Francisco: p. 8t; © Parade Publications, Inc., New York (Ayn Plant): p. 8b; Tony Stone Worldwide, München: p. 9t (Paddy Eckersley); p. 81 (David Maisel); p. 87 (Luciana Pamplone); © Jürgen Kleine, Ammerbuch: p. 9b; Mauritius, Stuttgart (Ley): p. 10; Martin Honeysett from *The World's Greatest Dad Cartoons* ed. by Mark Bryant, Watford: Exley Publications Ltd, 1992: p. 11; Jerrican, Paris (© Chantal Wolff): pp. 12, 78; *The New Yorker:* pp. 17 (23 January, 1995), 70 (21 November, 1994); by permission of the artist, © Michael Heath: p.18; Punch (used by permission of Erika Lüning and Renate Beitsch, Lübeck): p. 20; © Penguin Books: p. 21; Peanuts © 1996 United Feature Syndicate, Inc. Reprinted by permission: pp. 27, 84; © Ernst Klett Verlag, Stuttgart, Germany: p. 30; © HarperCollins, London: p. 31; © by Lois Lowry, Houghton Mifflin Company Boston, MA: p. 32; Riddell, *The Observer,* 25 June, 1995: p. 51; Cinetext Bild & Text Archiv GmbH, Frankfurt: pp. 36, 37, 39, 47;© Lucasfilm Ltd.: p. 38; Michael Wiese Productions: p. 40; © Miramax Books: p. 41; © Buena Vista Home Entertainment Inc., p. 44; Embassy Pictures Corp. and Lawrence Turman Inc.: pp. 48–49; p. 52; Don McPhee, *The Guardian,* 28 March, 1994: p. 53; Voller Ernst, Berlin (Dostal): p. 67; Deutsches Institut für Filmkunde, Frankfurt: p. 72; © Demart pro arte B.V., VG Bild-Kunst, Bonn 1996: p. 74; Angermayer, Holzkirchen: p. 83; dpa, Frankfurt/Main (Oliver Multhaup): p. 88; Bilderberg, Hamburg (Frieder Blickle): p. 93; © *The Spectator,* 29 July, 1995, by permission of the artist, Michael Heath: p. 97; © Rich Tennant: p. 99

Acknowledgements

The editors wish to thank all authors, publishers and literary agencies who have given permission to use copyright material. Sources are given underneath the texts. The following list acknowledges copyright holders who are not identical with the publishers quoted and also includes additional specifications demanded by copyright holders.
Every effort has been made to trace owners of copyright material, but in a few cases this has not proved possible and repeated enquiries have remained unanswered. The publishers would be glad to hear from any further copyright owners of material reproduced in this book.

P. 7: From "What's My Style?" by David Nunan, 1997 in David Gardner and Lindsay Miller (Eds.) *Tasks for independent language learning* (pp. 3–5). Copyright © 1997 by Teachers of English to Speakers of Other Languages, Inc. Excerpts from p. 4 adapted with permission; pp. 12–14: Reprinted by permission of HarperCollins *Publishers* Ltd (Bell & Hyman, an imprint of HarperCollins *Publishers* Limited); pp. 18–19: © *The Observer;* pp. 21–26: "Mildred" by Colby Rodowsky, copyright © 1989 by Colby Rodowsky. From *CONNECTIONS: SHORT STORIES* by Donald R. Gallo, Editor. Used by permission of Delacorte Press, a division of Bantam Doubleday Dell Publishing Group, Inc.; pp. 28–29: © Joan Lingard, 1987. Publishers Hodder & Stoughton; pp. 30–31: © Berlie Doherty, 1991; pp. 32–33: © 1993 by Lois Lowry. Houghton Mifflin Company, Boston, MA; pp. 34–35: *The War Between the Classes* Copyright © 1985 by Gloria D. Miklowitz. Veröffentlicht mit Genehmigung Nr. 61592 der Paul & Peter Fritz AG in Zürich; pp. 41–43: © Matt Damon and Ben Affleck; pp. 45–46: © Roger Ebert; pp. 47–48: Reprinted with the permission of Constable & Robinson Publishing; pp. 48–49: © Buck Henry, Lawrence Turman Inc.; pp. 63–66: "Playing God" by Ouida Sebestyen, copyright © 1987 by Ouida Sebestyen. From *VISIONS* by Donald R. Gallo, Editor. Used by permission of Dell Books, a division of Bantam Doubleday Dell Publishing Group, Inc.; pp. 72–73: reprinted by permission of the Walt Disney Company (Germany) GmbH; pp. 82–83: Copyright © 1991 by Peter Hedges. Veröffentlicht mit Genehmigung Nr. 53780 der Paul & Peter Fritz AG in Zürich; pp. 84–86: © Sue Hercombe and Peter Scott 1989. Reprinted from *New Plays 3* edited by Peter Terson (1988) by permission of Oxford University Press; p. 95: *You have the skills*, from *Oxfam UK and Ireland leaflet*, reproduced with permission of Oxfam, 274 Banbury Road, Oxford, OX2 7DZ. In Germany contact Oxfam Geschäftstelle, Georgenkirchstraße 70, 10249 Berlin; p. 100: © *The Observer;* pp. 104–105: From PIGEON FEATHER AND OTHER STORIES by John Updike. Copyright © 1962 by John Updike. Reprinted by permission of Alfred A. Knopf, a Division of Random House Inc.
The poems on pp. 74–75 are taken from the following sources: "To the Virgins, to Make Much of Time" from *The New Golden Treasury of English Verse,* London: Pan Books, 1980, p. 111; "Vitae Summa Brevis Spem Nos Vetat Incohare Longam" and "Ending" from *Short and Sweet Vol. 1*, ed. Alan Maley, London: Penguin, 1993, pp. 66 & 65.